Enjoy!

Ralph Welsh

BOMBS AWAY! Volume II

BOMBS AWAY!
Volume II

ANTHOLOGY OF B-17 AND B-24 BOMBING MISSIONS AND OTHER STORIES AND ILLUSTRATIONS RELATED TO THE LIFE, TIMES, PERSONNEL OF WORLD WAR II

RALPH WELSH, AUTHOR AND AGENT

Laura Joakimson, Editor

Contents

His Bravery Was No Act

Randolph E. Schmid, Associated Press

WASHINGTON—Lots of actors play war heroes on the screen. James Stewart was one in real life. A decorated World War II bomber pilot who returned from battle to star in *It's a Wonderful Life*, Stewart has been commemorated on a 41-cent postage stamp that was recently released. Stewart served in the 445th BG, 453rd BG and 3rd Combat Wing of the 8th Air Force. He flew twenty bombing missions over Germany, including one over Berlin, after wangling combat duty when commanders would have preferred to use a movie star for morale-building work at home. As a squadron commander, Stewart flew many dangerous missions when he could have sent others instead, recalled Robbie Robinson, a sergeant who was an engineer-gunner in Stewart's B-24 squadron. But while Stewart rose to colonel during the war and later retired as a brigadier general in the reserves, he didn't stand on ceremony.

Robinson, of Collierville, Tennessee, recalled one time when a creative tail gunner managed to "liberate" a keg of beer from the officers' club. That evening, Stewart wandered into a hut where some men were resting, picked up a cup, walked over to the "hidden" keg, poured himself a beer and sat back and drank it slowly, relaxing in a chair. "We were shaking in our boots," Robinson said. But Stewart merely got up, wiped out the cup, asked the men to keep an eye out for a missing keg of beer, and left.

Another time, Robinson recalled in a telephone interview, his plane landed behind another that was stuck on the end of the runway, nearly clipping its tail. After watching this, Stewart rubbed his chin and commented: "Ye gods, sergeant, somebody's going to get hurt in one of these things."

"Once in your lifetime, someone crosses your path that you could never forget, and that was Jimmy Stewart," Robinson concluded.

Dedicated in ceremonies at Universal Studios, Hollywood, California, this was the 13th stamp in the "Legends of Hollywood" series. A separate ceremony was held at the Jimmy Stewart Museum in Indiana, Pennsylvania, the actor's hometown. "It's our privilege to pay tribute to James Stewart, a fantastic actor, a great gentleman, a brave soldier, and an inspirational human being who truly led a wonderful life," Alan C. Kessler, vice chairman of the postal governing board, said in a statement.

Other highlights from Stewart's career include the movies *Rear Window, Vertigo,* and *The Man Who Knew Too Much,* all directed by Alfred Hitchcock.

Stewart played a country lawyer in *Anatomy of a Murder* and played a lawyer again in *The Man Who Shot Liberty Valance,* a western.

He won an Oscar for best actor in *The Philadelphia Story* in 1940.

Stewart died at age 89 on July 2, 1997.

When an Enemy

Was a Friend

Air Force Magazine *January 1997*
Copied from Eighth Air Force Historical Society—
Colorado Chapter Newsletter – B17-379th BG

A remarkable story of a Mission that started off from an airfield at Kimbolton, and ended at Seething airfield sixty years ago, or should we say in America in 1990. Brown's B-17 was perhaps the most heavily damaged bomber to return from combat. It survived because of an enemy's act of chivalry.

December 20th, 1943, was a typical overcast day in Britain as 2nd Lt. Charles L. Brown's B-17F lined up for takeoff. It was 21 year old Charlie Brown's first combat mission as an aircraft commander with the 379th Bomb Group at Kimbolton, England. The target was an FW-190 factory at Bremen, Germany. He and his crew of "Ye Old Pub" were to become participants in an event probably unique at that time in the air war over Europe, a mission that would remain shrouded in mystery for many years.

The bombers began their ten-minute bomb run at 27,300 feet,

the outside temperature—60 below. Flak was heavy and accurate. Before "Bombs Away," Brown's B-17 took hits that shattered the Plexiglas nose, knocked out the number four, which frequently had to be throttled back to prevent over speeding, and caused undetermined damage to the controls. Coming off target, Lt. Brown was unable to stay with the formation and became a straggler.

Almost immediately, the lone and limping B-17 came under a series of attacks from twelve to fifteen Bf-109s and FW-190s that lasted for more than ten minutes. The number three engine was hit and would produce only half power. Oxygen, hydraulic, and electrical systems were damaged and the controls were only partially responsive. The bomber's eleven defensive guns were reduced by the extreme cold to only the two top turret guns and one forward firing nose gun. The tail gunner was killed and all but one of the crew in the rear incapacitated by wounds or exposure to the frigid air. Lt. Brown took a bullet fragment in his right shoulder.

Charlie Brown's only chance of surviving this pitifully unequal battle was to go on the offensive. Each time a wave of attackers approached, he turned into them, trying to disrupt their aim with his remaining firepower. The last thing the oxygen-starved Brown remembers was reversing a steep turn, becoming inverted, and looking "up" at the ground. When he regained full consciousness, the B-17 was miraculously level at less than 1,000 feet.

Still partially dazed, Lt. Brown began a slow climb with only one engine at full power. With three seriously injured aboard, he rejected bailing out or crash landing. The alternative was a thin chance of reaching the UK. While nursing the battered bomber toward England, Lt. Brown looked out the right window and saw a Bf-109 flying on his wing. The pilot waved, then flew across the

B-17s nose and motioned Lt. Brown to land in Germany, which the aircraft commander refused to do. After escorting them for several miles out over the North Sea, the Luftwaffe pilot saluted, rolled over, and disappeared. Why had he not shot them down? The answer did not emerge for many years.

The B-17 did make it across 250 miles of the storm-tossed North Sea and landed at Seething near the English coast, home of the 448th Bomb Group which had not yet flown its first mission. The crew were debriefed on their mission, including the strange encounter with the Bf-109. For unknown reasons, the debriefing was classified "secret" and remained so for many years. Lt. Brown went on to complete a combat tour, finish college, accept a regular commission, and serve in the Office of Special Investigations with the Joint Chiefs of Staff, and in other Air Force and State Department assignments until his retirement. He now lives in Miami, Florida, where he is a founder and president of an energy and environmental research center.

The image of this strange encounter with the Bf-109 remained firmly embedded in Charlie Brown's memory. In 1986, he began a search for the anonymous pilot. Finally, in 1990, former Oberleutnant Franz Stigler, now living in Canada, responded to a notice published in a newsletter for German fighter pilots. By comparing time, place, and aircraft markings, it was determined that Stigler was the chivalrous pilot who had allowed Brown's crew to live. Not surprisingly, Brown and Stigler have become close friends.

On that December day, 1942, there had been two persuasive reasons why Stigler should have shot down the B-17. First, earlier in the day, he had downed two four-engine bombers and needed only one more that day to earn a Knight's Cross. Second, his decision to not finish off the aircraft was a court martial offense in Nazi Germany and if revealed could have led to his execution. He considered these alternatives while flying formation with the B-17, "the most heavily damaged aircraft I ever saw that was still flying." He could see the wounded aboard and thought, "I cannot kill these half-dead people. It would be like shooting at a parachute."

Franz Stigler's act of chivalry has been justly, though belatedly, honored by several military organizations in America and abroad. On the other hand, Charles Brown was not decorated for his heroism over Germany, which was never reported by the 448th Bomb Group at Seething to his Commanders. Such are the fortunes of war and its aftermath.

Author's note: My thought is that the mission briefing was classified "secret" to protect the German pilot. Germany had an excellent intelligence network.

448th Bomb Group

Profiles

George DuPont

Although Military regulations prohibited keeping animals, there were always a few who managed to find a stray dog or two. As crews passed through places like Belem and Marrakesh, they also found ways to collect other animals such as the Spider monkey.

One such monkey made it half way across the South Atlantic before a joyful urge compelled him to jump out the waist gunner's window. (He was not seen again.)

Another such monkey with better manners made it to England. "Flak" as he was called was not your ideal house guest. Anything on a shelf or left unattended was at your peril. Among some of his more notable bizarre escapades was jumping onto a red hot stove (much to his chagrin) and eating a whole can of cheese from our "K" rations. The cheese weighed half as much as he did. The results were almost final. Only the love of a friendly medic (who gave him and an enema with an eye dropper) saved him. He was adopted by a radio operator who (using a razor) cut an oxygen mask down to fit him. He carried Flak on his missions, keeping him warm between his heated suit and his sheepskin jacket.

He made quite a sight peeping out of the jacket, only his beady eyes and furry head visible through the open zipper.

As the fates would have it, people were more concerned about Flak than whether the target was hit.

One day Fate terminated his career. Two bombs failed to release and the radio operator (forgetting about Flak) stepped into the bomb bay with a screwdriver and started prying the lower bomb latches loose. At this moment he caught sight of Flak sitting on the fins of the top bomb. Just as he reached up to grab him, both bombs fell away with Flak still attached.

When things got dull around the bar racks someone would remark, "Boy, I'll bet if the Germans saw him they'd think we had guided missiles," or "I wonder if Flak ever let go?" To which another would add, "No way, he was too smart for that."

M/Sgt. Alexander was a hard working dedicated crew chief. I remember the pride he felt when he learned that our base Colonel Mason was to fly his aircraft and lead the formation. He and his crew labored all night to fine-tune the engines and then, to complete their task, used buckets of varsol and mopping away every evidence of crude and mud had the aircraft as shining as a new dime. It actually glowed in the misty dark.

Col. Mason noticed it too and approaching M/Sgt. Alexander asked politely, "Don't you like me sergeant?" Puzzled Alexander replied, "What do you mean?"

"Come with me," he motioned and walking across the perimeter he pointed to all the other dirty, dingy aircraft and said, "Sergeant, if you were a German fighter pilot and you saw this aircraft glistening in your eyes, wouldn't you want to *put out the light*? I want my aircraft to look like every other aircraft!" The sergeant and his crew mixed some mud with varsol and re-washed the aircraft to make it look dirty and dingy.

Not a Happy New Year's Day

Julian K. Wilson, 453rd

The following is taken from the Station 144 report filed on 4 January 1945. Subject: Mission # 197, 1 January '45, Target: Remagen.

The marshalling was very slow due to the fog. The takeoff was a nightmare. The visibility was never over 100 yards. There were five pots placed on the right side of the runway to assist the copilot in keeping visual contact. The first ship was off a little to the left of the runway as it passed the end. The second ship, Lt. Putman, made a good takeoff. The third ship, Lt. Judd, made a sharp left turn, went through the 732nd hardstand area, took the tail off WHAM-BAM, the wing off another ship, and cracked up just outside the of the 732nd area. The next four ships all went to the left of the runway. Capt. Lutes drug a wing on takeoff and Lt. Stout took over and flew the aircraft off. One aircraft started to take off and when the pilot felt the aircraft running over rough ground he chopped the power and got the aircraft stopped to the left of the runway about 100 yards. The tower controller at the upward end of the runway could neither see nor hear this aircraft although it was not over 100 yards away.

This is an excerpt from a document classified at the time as "Secret":

"Judd leading off in #65 veered left about halfway down the runway. His wheels clipped the tail off WHAM-BAM as the plane started to climb. Even then he might have remained airborne were it not for another ship parked in the path of the oncoming and partially stalled #65. When Judd's wheel hit the wing of the parked plane, #65 flopped over on her back, hurtled forward until a tree stopped the remaining momentum... Two men lived through the disaster miraculously enough: S/Sgt. Walter E. Beck, waist gunner, and Lt. Frank Pitcovich, pilotage navigator. Beck's condition is very serious, while outside of a few broken bones, Pitcovich got out with a bad case of shock. It was a sudden finish of a crew whose average age was 19, and which in the past month had really earned a fine reputation for outstanding ability...Only six ships got off that day—two from the 735th. Schauerman made a normal takeoff while Garrett, on his last mission, left the runway at approximately the same point as Judd. How he managed to stay in the air with a full bomb load will remain one of the unsolved miracles of combat operations."

Garrett has written about the events of January 1, 1945 from the standpoint of what he was doing that day, titling his paper (unpublished to this date) "The Bulge, The Bridge, and Bodenplatte." I have the approval of Bill Garrett to include the direct quotes used in this story taken from his paper.

A number of persons still active in the 453rd Bomb Group Association will recall the events of this day as well. They include the 735th Engineering Officer, Harry Godges.

Harry Godges has maintained a logging of the operational status for each of the aircraft assigned to the 735th Squadron. Tom Brittan has similarly compiled a record of the history of each specific ASN numbered B-24 assigned to the 453rd.

After the war, Don Olds, the person who must be credited with being the active motivating force in collecting the original nucleus of the members of the 453rd together as an association, collaborated with General Andrew Low to produce the first record of the history of the 453rd outside of the microfilms in which the group history had been imbedded. In order to do this, they had gleaned the official records of daily reports filed during our operational period at Old Buckenham, Station 144. This was supplemented by memoirs held by General Low of his days at Old Buck.

Data from each of the above references are combined in the following story. Fact is the backbone of what could be read as fiction by most any reader.

The following is a recreation of the scene on that morning of January 1, 1945. All quoted text, written by William Garrett, is excerpted out of context.

"At about 0600 we received our first information as to where we were going and what we were to attack. We then picked up our parachutes, emergency kits, maps, and "flimsy" (paper with code words, call signs, colors of the day for flares, control points and radio frequencies and channels for various target and weather information) and catch assigned trucks which carried us to the hardstands where our B-24s were dispersed over the airfield. We would arrive at our respective aircraft at least one hour before takeoff, which was scheduled that day to commence at 0805 hours."

"...The weather was a big problem all through the first few weeks of the Battle of the Bulge, and New Year's Day 1945 was no exception. There was heavy fog at Old Buckenham, with visibility at dawn of a maximum of 100 yards. There was snow on the field, and although the runways had been cleared of it, they were slick. It was a very cold morning. Incidentally, the Allies had converted to British summer time (from British double summer time) on 17 September 1944, and the Germans went back to middle European time on 2 October 1944. As a result, both sides used the same clock time during the entire battle..."

"...After checking out SQUEE-GEE with the crew chief, Master Sergeant Harold H. Fox, and his people, we set up our stations and gathered around the plane awaiting time to be at stations—ready to start engines. We would not have been surprised if the word had come that the mission was delayed or scrubbed because of the miserable visibility conditions. Due to the desperate struggle going on in the battle area, the decision was that we had to go—weather or no."

"... Our load of four M66 2,000 lb bombs on 1 January 1945 was the heaviest bomb load our crew ever carried. Previously we had carried three 2,000 lb bombs on 26 September 1944 when attacking a railway bridge over the Lippe Canal, on 4 November to the railway marshaling yards at Karlsruhe, and on 6 November to the Mittelland Canal Locks at Minden. Since these targets were deeper into Germany than Remagen, we had probably carried 2500-2700 gallons of fuel rather than the 2300 we were carrying to Remagen. This would explain, from a weight standpoint, the additional 2,000 lb bomb on our 1 January 1945 Remagen mission."

"... As we taxied out to the main runway 26 in the fog, I detected what I thought was a bit greater visibility—perhaps more than a football field, a bit greater than when at our hardstand 23 nearby. On the way to takeoff position (we were seventh in line) we were stopped longer than what was normal for such a procedure. It seemed to me—perhaps it was wishful thinking—that visibility was increasing slowly. I thought I might be able to make a visual takeoff. I told my copilot to keep a sharp lookout from his right seat window at the edge of the runway and let me know quickly if we were moving towards or away from it."

"...When I received the green light to go (we were on radio silence as the Luftwaffe Horchdienst, their Y service, was listening), I made a carrier type departure—brakes fully engaged while the throttles were advanced to the stops and the electronic supercharger was set at position 8. This was standard takeoff power with flaps set at 20-degree position. When the engines seemed to be running at full power, with the propellers at high RPM (2700), I released the brakes and we began the takeoff roll."

"...The takeoff made on 1 January 1945 will remain in my memory, vividly, as long as I live. The smaller details, considering it occurred more than fifty years ago, are hazy, though the broader event itself will haunt me as long as I live. I had made a full instrument takeoff in similar dense fog on 19 December 1944 without any problem. I should have attempted the same on 1 January 1945. I recall SQUEE-GEE, upon release of brakes, rolling forward, slowly at first, but accelerating with alacrity, heading out along the 26 track. Rapidly glancing back and forth, ahead at the directional gyro and saw that the 26 was not centered. As I attempted to bring it back to center, I felt SQUEE-GEE jolt and bounce, which made it clear that she was off the runway to the left. I immediately twisted the electronic turbo control to the "10" position from the standard position of "8" on takeoff. This was "War Emergency Power" which drove the manifold pressure from 48 inches to about 56 inches of mercury. There was an immediate surge of power setting before... this was a power setting for a dire emergency only, that it could be used for five minutes maximum...

SQUEE-GEE was pulled or lifted off the ground with an airspeed of 120-130 miles per hour. We were in dense fog with nothing visible ahead or to the sides. Gear was retracted and we began to gain altitude. In a few minutes we were out of the dense fog and into blinding sunshine."

"...The takeoff was a clear example of the excellence of the designers and builders of SQUEE-GEE, the superb Pratt and Whitney R-1830-65 radial engines, and the dedicated and conscientious maintenance by Master Sergeant Harold H. Fox and his ground crew. These factors and SQUEE-GEE overrode the handicap imposed on her by an impromptu procedure by me and rescued us from the consequences of my mistake."

Upon mission return:

"...When we landed we were met by the usual truck to take us to the standard debriefing procedure. A jeep also arrived, with, I believe, Lt. Col. Edward F. Hubbard, the Air Executive of the 453rd Bomb Group. He may have been accompanied by Lt. Col Van Dowda, who had just become Group Operations Officer. I recall being shown, as they drove me down runway 26, the still visible tracks of B-24 wheels going off the runway to the left (southwest). Some of these tracks were undoubtedly mine. I can't recall now how far from the takeoff position they began to go off to the left, but I believe it was near 4,000 feet down the runway. They identified Judd's tracks in the same area, and we drove to the latter's crash scene..."

"Ellingham, near Attleborough, Norfolk, England... Pat was an 11 year old schoolboy who lived near our base. He was walking on Abbey Road, along the south perimeter of our airfield, to Old Buckenham School when he came upon the wreckage of a B-24 blocking Abbey Road and his route to school. This was the B-24 piloted by Lt. Alan C. Judd, who had been scheduled to lead the high right squadron on (in which we were to lead the high right element that morning). This location is also verified by reports which state that Judd went off runway 26 to the left on takeoff and into the area of the 732nd Bomb Squadron hardstands which were just south of runway 26 and just north of Abbey Road. In the 732nd area, Judd's B-24 struck the tail of WHAM-BAM (our brightly painted formation and utility B-24D), took the wing off another parked B-24, and then ended up at Abbey Road where Pat Ramm encountered it... This crash was the cause of our delay in getting to takeoff position. Since we were on radio silence, we did not learn of this accident until we returned from the Remagen mission."

This is the end of Garrett's report.

After preparing this material, I felt I had accomplished two things:

(1) A person who had collected bits and pieces of the events involving the crash of her loved one, could now sort out and trash accounts that were not true, plus the true events assembled for her were now identified in their proper sequential series (except for the Station 144 report of 4 January 1945 at the opening of this article).

(2) A remarkable story has been brought to life that would have otherwise gone unpublished. This indeed was the case, and, now practically fifty-five years after the incident and almost five years since its writing, a small portion of the entire story is now seeing daylight!

One Day in the Life

of Aviation

Ordnance

Ben Hooker, 458th

It is late evening, May 7, 1944, and the second shift of 754th Ordnance is reporting for duty. The 754th is part of the 458th Bomb Group (H) stationed just outside Norwich, England. The ordnance office is a little cubicle located along the side of the big hangar near the control tower. As we enter, the clerk doesn't look up from his typewriter, for he knows that someone will ask the inevitable questions, "Have we been alerted?" or "What is the bomb load?" Most of the time he doesn't know any more than we do, so his answer is usually meant to deceive. If we can find out the type of bomb ordered we can speculate on the target, or at least the type of target.

As the day crew has cleaned up most of the work, a few of us drift down to flak suit storage under the pretext of checking their condition, but actually to goof off more than anything else. Someone decides he is hungry. We ante up the shillings required to send for a few pounds of fish and chips, and he slips out through a hole in the fence and comes back shortly with a bundle wrapped in a London or Norwich newspaper.

Flak suits are just about as popular with the air crews as car seat belts are now. Pilots (particularly new ones) usually sat on them until a heavy barrage ventilated the cockpit—then they had a change of attitude. It is our job to place one for every crew position.

At about 2200 hours the order comes down—the mission is on, and a lot of work by a lot of men is required this night before the big birds can fly. Of course we still don't know where the target is, but we later learn that it is Brunswick. Bomb load is 12 500 lb. GP, with M-103 nose and M-106 tail fuze, instantaneous. All crews mount their bomb service trucks (BST) and race to the bomb storage area. Since all four squadrons are vying to be first to load, there is some confusion and traffic congestion. After a wait that seems interminable, we are finally loaded with bombs, fins, fuses and other accessories required to put together a bang big enough to ruin Herr Hitler's day.

The big birds (B-24s of the 754th) are sitting on the hardstands waiting for the eggs to be loaded. Each bomb is moved by dolly to the bomb bay, hoisted and attached to the shackle, fused, arming wires attached, and safety pins checked and tagged. This is repeated until all aircraft are loaded. My notes indicate that AC #276 is already loaded from a previous mission, probably aborted. Normally if a mission is scrubbed all bombs must be removed and returned to storage, making double work.

Dawn is just breaking as we finish the last plane, and it won't be long until preflight and then the air crews show up for the day's business. We head for the mess hall and some hot chow, and then to the barracks for some "sack time."

I'm just barely asleep when one of the day crew awakens me to inform that one of the planes we just loaded has crashed and burned on takeoff. It is "Belle of Boston," AC #42-52404, and the pilot is Lt. Paul Kingsley, my cousin. I can't get back to sleep, so I sit on the side of my bunk and smoke a cigarette. I have previously witnessed crippled bombers come in and the customary red flare arcing skyward indicating wounded on board, but for the first time I'm really aware that people are being killed in this war.

I attend the military funeral for Lt. Kingsley at the Cambridge Military Cemetery, and later, when his body is brought back to the States I act as pall bearer at a second burial service.

Paul is buried in the same cemetery where my father and mother are laid to rest. When I visit the cemetery I invariably gaze at the 8th AF insignia on his grave marker and I'm transported in memory back to the date also inscribed there, May 8, 1944.

Over the Rainbow

William McGinley, 392nd

Our crew, commanded by Lt. Stukus, had arrived at Wendling on October 15, 1943 as one of the early replacement crews and had completed eight combat missions when, on January 29th, 1944, we were awakened in the very early hours for our ninth and what eventually turned out to be our last mission.

The primary target was Frankfurt, in central Germany. The misfortune began during the group's assembly over East Anglia when one of our ships, from the 577th Squadron, had a terrible midair collision, in cloud, with one of the 482nd Group's Pathfinder B-24s with one of our original 392nd crews on board. From the two ships, a total of only three men managed to escape from the tumbling wreckage of the Pathfinder and survive.

Due to those same clouds which extended all along our route, with a few breaks, we lost contact with our group's formation en route to Frankfurt. We decided to turn back when we failed to locate any other B-24s with which we could have joined up and so complete the mission as briefed.

Shortly after turning back, we came under attack by a swarm of German fighters and a running battle ensued for the next twenty minutes or so, in and out of the clouds at high altitude, but as our ship sustained and absorbed more damage we were forced down to 2,000 feet, losing altitude and on fire.

Our navigator and bombardier had been killed during the battle, our gunners were completely out of ammunition, and three German fighters were coming in fast and lining us up in their gun sights, so we survivors had no alternative but to bail out. I scrambled from the tail gun turret, went forward and hauled the ball gunner up from his plexiglass turret. After standing at the open waist exit door for a moment, absolutely terrified as I looked down at the open countryside slowly passing below, I jumped into space. I've never forgotten getting out of that burning bomber.

I had no idea where I was as I floated down and landed clumsily in an open, freshly plowed field. Quickly unbuckling my chute harness, I started running across the field, looking for a hiding place. As I was stumbling my way over the plowed furrows, I saw someone waving at me frantically at me from the edge of the field to get down and stay down.

Little did I know that this was my first contact with the Belgian resistance movement. I immediately flopped forward, face down on the soft soil, and checked my wristwatch. It was 1100 hours. I stayed as still as possible, face down and hugging the cold, damp ground while hearing the distant shouting and yelling from German patrols as they traveled along the surrounding country roads, tracks and through woodland searching for me and the other survivors from our crashed plane.

We'd been told back at Wendling that if we could manage to get through the first twelve hours in enemy-occupied territory without getting caught, there was a reasonable chance that the underground movement would make contact. I was very lucky, because as soon as it began to get dark a resistance member came for me.

I soon learned first-hand of the ingenuity, bravado and

courage of the resistance organization. They hid me, together with other crew members from our plane, in a small room built with wooden boards and corrugated iron, which had been dug underneath a haystack. The secret hiding place was beneath the closest haystack to the road. Their reasoning was that a very obvious hiding place would be the last one to be thoroughly searched, if at all.

The resistance kept us supplied with sufficient food and drink during our time in the hideout, visiting only after nightfall. Each and every time I heard an unfamiliar sound outside our haystack I had terrifying visions of Nazi soldiers stealthily approaching.

When the resistance decided the time was right for our next move, they made all the necessary arrangements for us to be issued forged documents, civilian clothes, and a guide to take us by train into the large, sprawling city of Brussels, Belgium.

I had just gotten off the train at the railroad station in Brussels and was making my way through the crowds of milling people when I saw a German soldier, in field-grey uniform, walking along the platform towards me. I kept changing direction to avoid him, but clumsily walked right into him. I can only speak English, so there wasn't anything I could say. Luckily, he just laughed. So I laughed and managed to smile. He then said something unintelligible. I could only smile weakly in response and saunter away, my heart beating wildly.

Months later, when I became more accustomed to my behind-the-lines status, I would even ride on the streetcars, occasionally sitting beside German soldiers. If I were captured, I would be sent to a prisoner-of-war camp until the end of the war. What really worried me was that if any of the resistance people, who were hiding me in the city and transferring me to various addresses in Brussels in order to avoid the suspicions of neighbors, were unfortunate enough to be captured, they would either be tortured for information and then shot, or shipped east to face the horrors of a concentration camp where death often came as a blessed relief. For this reason, the percentage of volunteers, especially those with children, involved in the highly dangerous work of the resistance organizations, was very low.

Of course, there were a few exceptions. One of the key members of the underground in Belgium was British-born Anne Brusselmans, a 39 year old mother of two. I first met Anne in a Brussels basement in February 1944. She played a leading part in looking after us and arranging our moves to different locations. An estimated 130 Allied airmen eventually found their way to freedom because of her efforts. On one occasion the Gestapo managed to infiltrate the resistance network and caught one of her friends harboring downed American airmen. The father of the family was shot and the rest went into concentration camps.

The resistance members in Holland, Belgium and France were truly heroic people and took tremendous risks. Jane, a courageous young woman after whom I subsequently named my daughter, was a typical example.

She had previously been caught and beaten once by the Gestapo, but hadn't cracked under extreme interrogation and was subsequently released after managing to convince them of her innocence. Jane, and two resistance men in German uniforms, would drive towards a specific border point where they tied her up. At the border crossing they'd say she was a prisoner being taken to France for questioning. When they wanted to get back into Belgium they'd use a different border checkpoint and drive through again.

I well remember the Belgian count was also a member of the resistance organization. He spoke fluent German, and, with forged ID documents, would go to an airfield wearing a Gestapo officer's uniform, complete with skull and crossbones insignia, and dine at the officers' mess. In the meantime, Louie, the count's chauffeur/handyman, who was a quite extraordinary character, would wander around the airfield wearing the uniform of a German private and pour sugar in the fuel tanks of their airplanes. They would do anything.

I had given my service number to the underground to notify the International Red Cross authorities, not realizing that Europeans use a small cross mark on the number seven and, because of this, an error was made in transmitting my number. Subsequently, all the figure 7s in my number were thought to be 1s, so without any underground or German confirmation of my status, the Red Cross reported me as dead. My mother, at home in Mabelvale, near Little Rock, Arkansas, was notified by our War Department as "missing in action," and then, a little later, as "killed in action." But she adamantly refused to accept that I'd been killed.

During the following weeks and months, I didn't know what was going on. Someone would come to the house where we were hiding and say, "Let's go," and we'd go. We didn't know because we were not supposed to know.

After months of hiding at various locations, I sat in a Belgian café and witnessed the German army in full retreat following the Allied invasion of France. It was really something to see. Thousands of German troops with their equipment (some of the trucks and staff cars were being hauled by horses due to lack of gasoline) jammed the road, barely moving, all heading towards Germany. I felt sorry for the plainly under-nourished horses, but had not the slightest sympathy for the soldiers.

After being reunited with the American forces as the Allies advanced across Europe, I was flown back to England in September 1944, and saw, from the air, the thousands of bomb and shell craters that marked the Allied advance from the Normandy beaches and extended back inland as far as the eye could see.

As we flew over the English Channel and the southern coast of England came into view, I vividly recall seeing one of the biggest and most beautiful rainbows ever created.

Paralyzed with Fear

Ken Jones, 389th

April 4, 1945—Parchim

German Airfield—Secondary Wesendorf

Aircraft K—567th BS

Flight Time 8:15 hrs.

Bomb Load 12-150 lb G.P.

The silver screen—hometown USA—A Sioux War Chief mounts his pony on the run. He gives a blood curdling war cry and shouts, "It's a great way to die."

At briefing we learn we are going to blast the German fighters where they eat their sauerkraut and wiener schnitzel, on the home field in northwestern Germany. Going to meet an ugly "widow maker" in the sunshine.

Flying Lead, Low Left Squadron of 389th Bomb Group. Visual takeoff from base. Some clouds predicted over target. 6/10s to 10/10s in some places.

Unopposed on penetration. A few black smudges of 88s out of range to let us know we are expected. Code word given for primary target visual. We started to uncover to trail the lead squadron at the group IP. While making this slow left turn, I looked down through an opening in the clouds and saw two

German fighters taking off from an airfield. Alerted gunners, "Bandits airborne."

One minute or less later, I saw a jet turbine ME 262 coming at us from 9 o'clock level and circling to our rear. I pulled the squadron in close. I don't know why I did it but we were slightly offset to the right of the lead squadron upon completion of the turn. The clock stopped ticking and we braced ourselves for the attack. This twin-jet "bomber destroyer" can punch out 96 lb of 30 mm cannon shells in one three-second burst.

The jet seemed to hesitate and overshot our portside. I think he was going for someone in our low squadron and he misjudged his turn. At a distance he was watching the lead squadron and thought our squadron would come out of the turn in line with the lead. The jet was faster than anything I have ever seen. Joe Walko, left waist gunner, saw him coming all the way and only got off a short burst of 21 rounds of ammo.

Untouched, the jet pulled up, climbing to the lead squadron, his speed falling off. He dropped his flaps, which had holes in them like a navy dive bomber. The Luftwaffe Sturmvogel jet was now flying at formation speed behind #6, B-24 X-, in the three plane element directly behind and below the lead ship. Jerry parked there with his motor running, about 200 yards out.

This action and the following events took place in seconds.

There was no screaming dive to attack with a few short bursts of firepower, followed by a fast, fading breakaway.

Jerry was reckless. He wanted to die—to be out of it. No one tried to help him.

Coming out of nowhere, the German pilot eased up behind X- with his engines idling. Up to this point he hasn't fired a single round of cannon shells. The tail gunner and X- spins his turret and lines up his twin fifties and the movement stops. The gunner does not fire his machine guns.

He sits there in disbelief. Time is suspended. Jerry is looking straight down the tail gunner's throat with four 30 mm canons. They stare at each other. The gunner is paralyzed with fear. The last thing the gunner will see is four orange flashes of light from the nose of the jet.

The tail turret shattered. Dissolved. The jet pilot touched his right rudder and fired short bursts. A real ace. The top turret and waist gunners on X- cannot bring their gun sights to bear on the German. Other gunners in the slot or bucket element did not fire their guns, apparently watching in fascination. Damn! I wish I had my squirrel rifle. I can hear someone screaming "Shoot... Shoot" into my oxygen mask.

The right stabilizer came off X- and came sailing down through our squadron, big as a barn door. I could see the impact of canon shell fire striking No. 3 engine and then shifting over to No. 2. Debris was flying off and sailing back into the slipstream. B-24 X- went into a flat spin, trailing smoke.

We were so close, I could see mud splattered on the fuselage of the German plane. The Luftwaffe pilot in the mottled colored jet popped his flaps and dove for the clouds. No shots were fired at him except from our plane on the way in. X- spun into the clouds and no chutes were seen by our gunners.

Like shooting fish in a barrel! I feel nauseated. Half anger and half fear. Maybe mostly fear that "there go I."

Completed bomb run and did not release bombs because clouds obscured the target. Lots of bandit chatter in the air dilutes the threat of flak bursting around us. Going full bore "at a walk" toward the rally point.

Code word given for the secondary target at Wesendorf. Made the IP and uncover from group formation to bomb by squadron. Looking for fighters. The bombardier can see the German airfield and I know we'll get this one visual. Just sitting there. Letting the auto-pilot and bombsight take us on in. Black stuff boiling up to meet us with an explosive welcome.

"Bombs Away" and let's get the hell out of here. Flak moderate to meager. Depends where you are on the dance floor when the band begins to play.

No such thing as an easy mission. If there is only one burst of flak and it gets you, it's a rough mission.

Second Combat Wing under fighter attacks, off and on for thirty-five minutes. Must be mostly green pilots, they don't seem too aggressive and we don't see anyone else go down. The fighter screen is very effective at keeping Jerry at bay.

Saw many enemy aircraft and dog fights. P-51s diving and climbing all over the sky. The Mustangs better keep their distance—the boys looking over 50 cal. machine guns are a little nervous.

One bomber, another group, had No. 3 on fire. Trailing flame and smoke. A cripple and a straggler. Falling back of his formation. Our navigator, Pat Patterson, praying out loud for them on the intercom. Finally, prayers answered, the fire went out. A straggler will attract lots of attention today.

The war gives you two choices; kill or be killed. Whether you are on the ground in a fox hole or 4 1/2 miles up in the sky, you get him or he gets you. It's impersonal and insane. You must decide ahead of time just how you would react. You can't call a "time out" while you think about it. You just do it.

Sudden death in the cold, rarefied atmosphere of altitude. A tear is shed for ten young men gone in the blinking of an eye and for those who lived to see it happen. The sky has no memory because of gravity. We can't place ten wooden crosses or a granite stone here as a memorial to lost comrades. No marker can be placed to say, "This is where it happened." A scar on the brain and a terse message, "Missing in Action" is all that remains.

Wesel, Germany: D-Day at the Rhine River, 24 March 1945

Lt. Harold Dorfman, 714 Sqdn 448th B.G.

We first learned of this impending mission on the morning of the 22nd. Three crews were taken over to Headquarters 20th Combat Wing at Hardwick and briefed on the coming event.

We were to form three lead crews in our Group. I was lead DR Navigator, with Lt. Voigt as the lead pilot for 714th squadron flying as high right squadron, eight planes. General Timberlake briefed us and told us to forget about it until it came off. We learned that the main spearhead of allied troops, commandos, parachutists and glider borne were going to cross the Rhine River just a mile north of Wesel. We were to follow them in at treetop altitude and drop supplies.

The night of the 23rd we were taken in to study the drop area models and maps. Now we knew it was coming off the following day. The route in and out was over friendly territory all the way. We labeled it a milk run, another sightseeing trip. Except for about five minutes at the drop area we would never be over enemy territory.

Briefing was at 05:30, take off at 09:30, 26 planes in total (9-9-8). No heavy flying clothing. Just Class B uniform and a light jacket, back parachute and no Mae West. Everything went as briefed right up to the IP altitude about 75 feet. All radio homing navigation aids to the target were out of action, visibility down to about two miles in the haze. We crossed the Rhine south of course and reached the southern dropping area for American equipment. However, we carried supplies for the British landing area about a mile and a half further north. So we turned north and dropped perfectly on target, the British troops had marked the drop area with a circle of downed gliders. We started a 270 degree right turn out. That's where hell started!

A large bullet hole, the size of a handball appeared in the skin (of the plane) alongside of me, probably a twenty mm shell. I dropped to the armored floor between the ammunition cans and landed on Lt. "Shabby" Shabsis the bombardier. Our faces were about eighteen inches apart from the nose window and we watched more holes appear in the glass from machine gun fire. We covered ourselves with our flak jackets. I expected a bullet in the face at any moment. I could hear and feel the machine gun bullets raking the bottom of our armor plate that we were laying on. Suddenly there was a loud whine of high pressure being released behind us. We looked back at the nose wheel tire. It had been hit, just about a foot from my rear end. Still the machine guns raked the nose. The hydraulic lines in the wheel housing were hit, red fluid came out over everything, including my chute, which was soaked. A shell exploded between the pilot's legs, but mercifully the direction was away from him.

However, the pilots' control cables were shot out. He lost control of the rudder, his controls were crippled. The thing that saved us was their snapping-on the autopilot which continued to work. We were at fifty feet all this time and still to clear 100 feet high electrical wires as we came out of the turn to re-cross Rhine River. By the grace of God did we get over that line of wires and out across to the friendly side of the Rhine. At debriefing, the top turret gunner swore that we went under the wires, if so we had only inches to spare. All this had taken about five minutes from drop time on the target to across the Rhine. We were now out.

Col. Heber Thompson riding as Command Pilot alongside Lt. Voigt asked the tail gunner to report on the rest of the squadron. After a long delay, the answer was "Sir, there is nobody behind us." Seven planes vanished.

We had lost the entire squadron, seven planes, in the turn. This was bad news; later we learned that all seven had managed to get across to our side of the Rhine River and nobody was seriously wounded.

All our navigation instruments were shot out. No compass, no G Box. But at least we were alive and over friendly territory. We picked our way to Ostend by pilotage. The nose turret Pilotage Navigator got lost en route as we ran completely off his maps. I found our location on my map.

At Ostend, we decided to make for the RAF emergency field at Manston, two miles south of Margate on the southeast tip of England. We circled the field, checking our plane for thirty minutes and decided that the airplane was unfit to land. The tires were blown, the wheels wouldn't come down and the manual control cables were out. The autopilot, damaged in the turnout of Germany, would only make left turns and not to the right. The only manual control the pilots had was elevation, up or down. We were at 7000 feet. A case for bailing out or a gear-up landing. The bomb bays were open. I couldn't fit between the bomb racks with a backpack on and I'll be damned if I'd take it off. I grabbed hold of the racks, swung around them and back to the catwalk. Did that twice and then worked through the door down to the waist. Then the word came to "Bail Out" not "Crash Land." I tightened the leg straps on my chute and fastened them.

I knew that my chute was soaked with hydraulic fluid and might not open right away, if at all. It was a hell of a feeling. I was the second man to leave through the camera hatch. Seeing the first man fall clear gave me confidence, his chute opened immediately. I sat down by the hatch, leaned forward and tumbled out. That was something I never thought I could have the nerve to do, but they say if you gotta go, you gotta go.

It's hard to describe those first few seconds out. Tumbling aimlessly through nowhere. I wanted to see that airplane well clear of me before I pulled the ripcord. I looked for it and suddenly saw it well away from me. I was satisfied and pulled the ring. The cable came out about twelve inches and I waited, nothing happened. I was a little panicky, then I pulled it again. The cable came clear out. I waited again, this time for ages. Then it came, a sharp crack in the back of my neck and then a sudden jolt. There she was above me, just so beautiful and white. Not an angel, just a parachute, which at that moment was much better.

The jolt didn't hurt at all and I was comfortably floating. I don't think I have ever heard or rather been conscious of such peaceful quiet. The world was soundless and beautiful. A B-24 passed underneath with a slight hum and then it went quiet again. There is no sensation of falling, just drifting. I tried to remember what I had been taught about jumping and what I should do next.

I remembered that I should land with my back to the wind. I was facing the wrong way, so I reached up, twisted the shroud lines until I faced properly. I looked down and saw that I had quite an audience. I waved to some kids and they waved back. I was swinging badly at the bottom of my chute, but when I landed, luckily enough it was at the right part of the swing and I landed gently.

I don't even remember landing. I landed in a large field, behind a church, fairly smooth, with plenty of room on all sides. I looked up and counted ten chutes in the air. Everyone out OK. I was first to land. I cussed the loss of my hat when the chute opened. The people saw it come off my head and followed it down. Some kid ran off and got it for me, I gave him my gloves as a gift.

Several women ran toward me from the church obviously to welcome the returning hero, WRONG—they wanted my nylon parachute to make clothing!! I was forced to pull my gun and hold the ladies at gunpoint until an RAF Officer, jeep and driver arrived, collected the chute and explained to the ladies that I would have to pay for the chute if I didn't return it ($300). Then I made the ladies really mad when I showed them that the gun wasn't loaded. I pointed it at the sky and pulled the trigger and all you could hear was a meek "click."

I got RAF transport to Margate, had tea and then with the crew assembled returned to RAF Manston. All crew present and accounted for. Two injured in the jump. Colonel Heber Thompson landed on his face in a field with freshly fertilized manure, "Shabby" landed on his head and Reisinger on his face, but they weren't hurt seriously. Reisinger had swapped chutes with the radio operator, just before the jump because radio had spilled it while checking it. Reisinger jumped successfully with the spilled chute.

At Manston we found our C.O. Col. Westover with Capt. Wilhelmie. They had crash landed. Capt. Wilhelmie was shot in the leg and a gunner shot in the shoulder. Two planes came down from Seething to pick us up. The one that collected us up circled Seething for about twenty minutes and then advised us that we may have to bail out because he was not getting a "gear down" indication. I said "OK" as long as his crew would be kind enough to swap their well packed chutes for our slightly used ones. He managed to land the plane.

We were home, it was 7 pm. It had been a busy day, but it is not over. I took my camera, got on my bike headed for the flight line to photograph the damage on the planes that had returned. The hand brakes on my front wheel jammed. I flew over the wheel, landed on my right face and shoulder in a ditch. They loaded me into an ambulance, took me to the hospital, and with my face covered with bandages, put me to bed with the rest of the crew. Every member had some injury and qualified for the Purple Heart except me. I didn't have a mark on me except for the dumb bicycle accident.

Mission No. 18: "D" Day, June 6, 1944

Mac Meconis, 466th BG

Of the whole air force our group was to be the second to hit the beach. We had to be at certain places exactly at certain times in order to hit the invasion coast at the precise moment. With thousands of other bombers in the air at the same time, we had to be on schedule. Night flying normally is bad enough for the risks of collision, but this was different—every plane on English soil probably would be up there milling around in the soup. And soup it was before briefing time. It looked like good weather to cancel a mission.

More detailed information of the magnitude of the assault was given us. We learned that the attack by air would cover 25 miles of coast between Cherbourg and Le Havre, and that paratroops would land back of the coastal defense area. Our target secondary was a choke point in a road going through a wood near the coast.

En route we glimpsed something of the tremendous force of planes that were taking part in this assault. Everywhere, no matter in which direction you looked, formations large and small were on their way—all headed south, toward the setting moon. As we passed over the southern coast of England I began straining my eyes to see some of the invasion fleet. A low under cast in patches obscured most of the water, but wherever open spaces permitted I could see the landing craft and large ships on a fairly rough sea. Also below us, just above the clouds, I saw B-26 formations assembling. Didn't see a single friendly fighter, though we were expecting 35 squadrons as cover. They probably were at low altitude, below the clouds, actively aiding the first assault on the coast. We didn't need them.

The invasion coast appeared momentarily; we saw the artillery fire; and seconds later the top cloud layer was directly under us, drawing the white curtain on the show we'd hoped to see from our grandstand seats. PFF ships ahead dropped their bombs, and our bombs were away on their marker trails at 6:12 a.m. We'll never know exactly what we hit.

It was daylight, with the sun shining above the clouds in the east, as we turned right to head 270 degrees for ninety miles until we were west of the Cherbourg peninsula. Several bursts of flak came up at a group on our right just after bombs away. Later, as another group passed too close to either Cherbourg or the islands just west of it, a ball of flak like that I'd seen over Brunswick once, came up at them.

Another mission had taken off just before we landed back at base, so we expected to fly sometime in the afternoon. We left all our equipment at the plane and went to breakfast before going back to bed. I had a terrible headache and a gaseous stomach from fatigue and engine noise. Smith had appropriated our radio and newscasts said our troops were ten miles inland already.

Fact or Fiction?

One of the Spitfires, during the war, had a very odd passenger carried on it. (Not in it). It was common practice to have someone sit on the tailplane whilst the airplane was taxiing along the perimeter track in order to keep the tail on the ground. In this case it was a WAAF (lady airwoman), Margaret Horlton sitting on the fuselage facing backwards, with her legs jammed under the tailplane. The plan was for the pilot to stop at the end of the runway, allowing her to jump off. The pilot forgot she was on there and took off before she could do that. He reported to the tower that he had a very heavy tail trim, and he was instructed to fly low past the tower and they would have a look see. They told him not to panic, but he had a WAAF passenger on the tail. After completing one circuit of the airfield the pilot did land safely and let off a very frightened lady. I met this lady some years ago at an air show. The Spitfire was flown in for her to see, the press and TV were there to cover her reunion with the aircraft. She was invited to sit on the tail again. The aircraft was in the hangar, and she agreed to do so, provided that the hangar doors were closed. I did speak to her about her flight and she said she was terrified, but she seemed to think the pilot was suffering more from the shock than herself.

(As reported by Dick Wickham, December 2000 Station 146 Tower Assn., Seething Airfield, Norfolk.)

Author's note: I vote fiction.

How We Spent V-E Day

Ralph Elliott

As printed in the Gilman (Ill.) Star in July 1945 B-17, 467th BG

I thought perhaps it might be of some interest to the folks there to hear how several thousand of us in the Eighth Air Force spent V-E Day. (Actually both May 7 and May 8). We had been expecting the end of the war for some time, since our bombing came to an end several days ago. Even then we had to go way down to the Alps to find targets. So we knew the end was coming shortly and were "sweating it out" the same as everyone else.

In the last two and a half years the Eighth has unloaded ton after ton of bombs. In France, after it was liberated, we got to see some of our results. Air fields had been put out of use, refineries burned out, and factories were well wrecked. However, we knew that the devastation still didn't compare with the area along the Rhine River and in the Ruhr Valley.

Then, just before V-E Day, plans came through from higher headquarters to allow us to "tour" the Rhine area with ten ground men per ship as passengers. You can well imagine we were looking forward to it, and it turned out just as planned, only better.

The morning of May 7 found twenty-four skeleton bomber crews—pilot, copilot, navigator, engineer and radio operator—plus nearly two hundred and forty officers and enlisted men of our ground personnel assembled for briefing. Takeoff time was 1200 (noon) and as usual we made our times good, thirty seconds between ships off the runway.

I was leading the first three-ship element, and by the time we crossed the coast out of England both of my wing-men (Jones & Ercegovac) were in position. They both flew wide on this trip so that they could show their passengers anything they happened to see of special interest.

We crossed the Belgian coast at Ostend at 1000 feet and, as the weather was beautiful, visibility was perfect. It remained so all day. There were still a few old bomb craters visible, but little damage had been done.

Our route took us over Bruges, Brussels, and Ghent and we went over the center of each. We knew by then it was V-E Day because there were flags on everything; the black, yellow, and red of Belgium, the French Tri-color, the Stars and Stripes, the Union Jack, and half a dozen I couldn't recognize. All the big smoke stacks were covered and store- fronts were a blaze of color. Where all the flags came from I'll never know; maybe they'd been hidden during the occupation.

Our route took us from Ghent and Brussels across the German border near Luxembourg, on down to Mannheim. At the German border we could see the "dragon's teeth" of the Siegfried Line, and every so often we passed burned out tanks and trucks. We could tell where a fight had taken place from the tank tracks in the fields and the holes where the tanks had dug in. Some hills had bomb craters on them where medium or fighter-bombers had helped out—which side they helped we couldn't know. The country across Belgium is quite flat, but as we got into Germany it began to get hilly and proved to be well wooded. There weren't many good roads with the exception of the famous German Autobahns and those are really good. Most of them are four-lane highways with a wide grass strip down the middle. They seemed to have been little damaged and we saw plenty of traffic (ours) on them.

The first big German city we saw was Mannheim, one of the Eighth AF main targets. The railroad marshalling yards had been largely repaired but the houses near the yards were a mess. Fifty percent of the city will have to be rebuilt, I should guess. Just south of Mannheim lies the old German university city of Heidelberg. We missed it this trip, but I saw it several weeks ago and it is little damaged.

Next "stop" was Hanau, also badly hit. When you remember that this route covered the main industrial area of Western Germany, you get the feeling the "mess" has only begun and our feeling really proved correct. We flew down through a valley from Hanau to Frankfurt, following an autobahn and a railway, and we were hardly prepared for what we saw as we swung in over the city.

The Main River runs through the center of town, but to get from one side to the other must require a bit of swimming, because all of the bridges were down and not even a footbridge was left. Some were completely demolished, and others had just one span blown out at each end. Very likely the Germans had done that. The main railway station was in the center of the city and was as big as any in Chicago. However, the resemblance ended there, because this one had no roof on it. We circled at about 500 feet and it all appeared as a blackened mess of steel girders. All of the rail cars were burned out, and even the repair crews couldn't make it look normal again.

This time the whole city was plastered with craters and

nearly every house was badly damaged. It rather amazed us to see a big, modern apartment building still standing and in good condition among all the rubble. However, we saw things like that many times and couldn't help but wonder at it. As we followed the Main River up to where it emptied into the Rhine we saw more evidence of heavy bombing, and, from there on up, the Rhine was filled with sunken barges and river steamers. At one place only the two funnels of some tug were out of the water.

We passed Mainz and Wiesbaden past wrecked bridges and factories and turned north at Bingen where hills rose sharply and almost caught me too low. I banked steeply and headed down the river with hills rising on both sides of us, and I soon had to climb several hundred feet to make the bends in the river. That stretch up to Koblenz was the most beautiful I saw all day. The banks were steep and thickly wooded and on either side were old medieval castles. Some were old ruins covered with vines and bushes, but others were well kept. I couldn't help but wish I could land for a few hours and see some of those places closer.

At Koblenz the hills dropped sharply away again to a nearly level plain with factories on both sides of the river. I had seen the city before, but under not nearly so pleasant circumstances. I remembered a certain bridge at Koblenz and took a good look at where it HAD been. The day we went over at 20,000 feet I never expected to go back—or wanted to. In this whole area we saw the flak gun emplacements, and some of the guns were still there with their muzzles pointed upwards. To tell the truth, it almost gave me chills to remember those guns a few months before when I'd seen the muzzle flashes and counted the black puffs as the shells went off—until they got too thick to count and the smell of the black powder floated up into the bomb bays.

Downstream we flew over several prisoner camps, and the men looked like ants against the bare, sandy ground. There were too many to even guess at but there were several thousand of them. They had a few tents for shelter, but most of them looked like they all had were the clothes they wore. We were keeping our eyes open for the Ludendorff Bridge at Remagen as I had a photographer riding in the waist, and he wanted a good picture of it. (Capt. Calvin Horn, head of the camera shop, was the photographer.) I dropped down to treetop level as we saw it coming up, and the picture he got is wonderful. The towers of the bridge at both ends are standing, but appear to have been well blackened by smoke. It gave us a thrill to see the American flag flying off the east end; the German side of the river, and to realize how great an action put it there.

After a sharp turn to avoid the hills above the east end of the bridge, we leveled out almost over Bonn and could see Cologne in the distance. We could pinpoint ourselves by the outline of the cathedral at Cologne, and in a few minutes, we were over the city. The cathedral was pictured in nearly all of the papers back when our troops first took the city. The devastation in the area around there is almost unbelievable. The main railway station stands only a few hundred feet from the cathedral and is completely destroyed. Not a house is left, including the ones just across the street from the cathedral, and yet the cathedral is but slightly damaged. The houses and buildings are just piles of stone, and just pieces of walls are left. Bomb craters are everywhere, and the only paths through the rubble have been cut by bulldozers. Burned out tanks could be seen in the streets, reminders of the fighting that took place there.

I dropped low again and made a steep turn around the cathedral at about fifty feet for a good camera shot. Then we headed on up to Dusseldorf on the south edge of the Ruhr, better known as "happy valley" or "flak alley." Many a bomber went down over the Ruhr, and the Eighth AF will never forget the place—ever. It just wasn't healthy.

Leaving the Ruhr and more bombed out factories, the navigator (Arnold Thompson) gave me a course to Antwerp, Belgium and for 40 or 50 miles we rode the border of Belgium and Holland. Again we saw flags in all the cities we passed, and when we spotted a celebration going on in some little Belgian town we circled back over it low and shot a bunch of yellow-red flares just to celebrate a bit ourselves. The people all waved and were apparently having a wonderful time. We kind of felt good about it all ourselves.

At Antwerp the streets were crowded, and a big parade was in progress so we helped that along too with most of the flares we had left. Then we headed home past Walcheren Island which you may remember hearing of. The Canadians and Germans had a big fight there and the Germans blew the dykes, flooding the entire island. Some of the houses on higher ground were apparently being lived in, but most were clear under water. It was mainly farm land and fields are visible under the water. The trees are dead from the salt water and a hundred years will probably not see the land used again.

Actually, it is hard to imagine the destruction we saw on that trip. But for the boys who had worked on the ground during the war, as well as the ones of us who have been over Germany before, it was a memorable trip. We all agreed that V-E Day wouldn't soon be forgotten by us, and for me it proved to be all the "celebration" that was needed.

Home? Well, I'm hoping just like several million other guys that we'll be there soon.

"The Gunner": The Passing Of An Incredible Era

Bud Conder, CMSGT USAF RET

The twilight has slipped away; the sun has set on the career of the Aerial Gunner. The last official flight of the Aerial Gunner has been completed. The Aerial Gunner has flown heroically into the pages of history aboard... a B-52G model Bomber, number 62595. This historic flight took place on 30 September at Castle AFB, CA. The Unit: The 328th Bombardment Squadron, of the 93rd Bombardment Wing, 15th Air Force.

The era of the Aerial Gunner began for the United States in 1917, during WWI.

John L. Cox, a member of the AFGA, wrote: "In the beginning, Man had no need for defense, because Man had no weapons. As time progressed, Man invented weapons and became his own enemy... by World War I, Man had evolved the airplane... Alas, they eventually began to shoot at each other during aerial flight. Thus was born the aerial defensive gunner."

During and since WWI, Aerial Gunners have done their share

of flying and fighting for national defense. In air to air combat, through five wars, their aircraft have advanced from the slow open cockpit biplane, to the jet powered B-52.

WWI produced four Aces, all then called "Observers," who manned rear cockpit machine guns, downing twenty-two aircraft.

Gunners were overlooked in most cases and were not credited with aerial kills, because the public was more enamored with the fighter pilot. In the Argonne Offensive during WWI, gunners on observation planes shot down fifty-five aircraft; bombers accounted for thirty-nine.

Gunnery technology improved between WWI and WWII; better sighting devices, better guns and ammo and more guns were added to the bomber aircraft.

One thing didn't change in WWII; the "glory" still went to the fighter pilot. The thousands of enemy fighters downed by gunners were counted as a "team" effort, rather than crediting individual gunners. The Air Force claimed that record keeping was too difficult.

In spite of all the hardships encountered during aerial combat, the gunners gave an admirable account of themselves... Eighth Air Force bombers claimed 6,259 enemy aircraft shot down or destroyed; 1,836 probable, and 3,210 damaged. Their records exceeded that of the fighter pilots. Other theaters show similar results.

Dr. William Wolf, in an article appearing in the Winter 1991 issue of the USAF Museums Friends Journal, tells of the deadly expertise of S/Sgt. Donald B. Crossley, the highest scoring gunner in WWII; next highest was Michael Arooth, also in the ETO. After him, S/Sgt. Benjamin F. Warmer, flying in the MTO. Also discussed were T/Sgt. Arthur Benko, flying in the Pacific theater and S/Sgt. John Quinlan flying in the ETO.

S/Sgt. Donald Crossley, a Virginian and a B-17 tail gunner,

flew combat with the 95th Bombardment Group of the 8th Air Force. On 11 May 1943, Don scored his first two "kills" while flying on the LITTLE LADY. On 13 June 1943, he downed two more fighter planes, as a crew member aboard the B-17 EASY ACES. On 25 July 1943, his count climbed again. On 12 August 1943, he added a double over Bonn, to bring his score to eleven victories. His last victory, the twelfth, came on his 22nd mission in September 1943. After his 25th mission he was assigned to instruct, but was killed from injuries suffered in a jeep accident.

Michael Arooth of the 379th Bombardment Group was credited with downing nine enemy aircraft.

T/Sgt. Thomas Dye scored eight "kills" while flying with the 351st Bombardment Group.

On 5 July 1943, S/Sgt. Benjamin F. Warmer (also known as the wild waist gunner), a member of the 99th Bombardment Group serving in the MTO, was credited with shooting down seven German fighter aircraft that single day, while flying over Sicily. Later, he downed two more, for a total of nine.

Johnny Foley, "Johnny Zero" as he was called, while serving in New Guinea during WWII, without ever firing a gun in his life, volunteered to replace an injured turret gunner on a Martin B-26. Johnny downed two Zeros on his first mission. Later he shot down five more enemy aircraft. He survived three crashes and completed thirty-two missions in the Pacific. In Europe, he flew 31 more missions as a bombardier.

T/Sgt. Arthur Benko, an Arizonian flying with the 387th Bombardment Squadron, 308th Bombardment Group, was the top scorer in the Pacific. Arthur, flying as a top turret gunner on a B-25, on 2 October 1943 shot down seven Zeros. Later, he shot down two more aircraft and was credited by 14th Air Force for nine more ground victories. T/Sgt. Benko was lost when shot down over Hankou.

S/Sgt. John Quinlan, the tail gunner on the famous B-17, the MEMPHIS BELLE (now stately displayed in a place of honor on Mud Island in Memphis, TN), downed five German aircraft. John volunteered for further combat and scored three more "kills" against the Japanese, flying on the B-29, the MARIETTA MISS FIT.

During the Korean War, (Police Action??), B-29 gunners were credited with twenty-seven confirmed "kills." An extremely remarkable feat since the crew "prop-job" B-29 was up against the soft MIG fighter.

In Vietnam, the first MIG "kill" was credited to S/Sgt. Samuel O. Turner, a tail gunner aboard B-52D, #60676, flying with the 307th Bombardment Wing, out of U-Tapao, Thailand.

At sunset, on 18 December 1972, Operation LINEBACKER II was launched, the most intensive bombing campaign since WWII. At 1945 hours, MIG KILLER ONE began its bomb run on Hanoi. The sixth bomber over the target, she was under heavy attack by SAM missiles. The bomb run lasted only 2 minutes; then after leaving the target, Turner's B-52 also came under enemy fighter attack. That night, S/Sgt. Sam Turner entered history books; he was the first bomber gunner to shoot down a MIG-21. His victory was witnessed and confirmed by M/Sgt. Lionel L. LeBlanc (a member of the AFGA).

In all there were five MIG-21 aircraft claimed by B-52 gunners during Operation LINEBACKER II, but only two were confirmed.

Six days later, on Christmas Eve, 24 December 1972, A1C Albert E. Moore, flying as the tail gunner on B-52D #55083, DIAMOND LIL, downed the second MIG-21. His "kill" was also confirmed.

In 1985, M/Sgt. Samuel O. Turner passed away, but his legacy is not forgotten, because B-52D #60676, MIG KILLER with a big red star painted on her side stands guard over the Memorial to Sam in

Heritage Park, Fairchild AFB, Washington. Old MIG KILLER was the last B-52D flying and was retired in October 1983.

It is interesting to note that the Call Sign for B-52D #60676 on the flight on 18 December 1972, was called RUBY III.

Ernie Pyle's Column on the St. Lo Air Raid—25 July, 1944

Ernie Pyle was one of the most famous of the war correspondents. His usual reporting site was on or near the front lines. He was in Normandy for the D-Day landings and was with the ground forces on 25 July 1944 when the 8th bombed the front lines. There were 1503 bombers and 561 fighters on this mission. 3395 tons of bombs were dropped by the heavies. This is his account of that mission:

"...A new sound gradually droned in our ears, a sound deep and all-encompassing with no notes in it—just a gigantic faraway surge of doom like sound. It was the heavies. They came from directly behind us.

"At first they were the merest dots in the sky. We could see clots of them against the far heavens, too tiny to count individually. They came on with terrible slowness. They came in flights of twelve, three flights to a group, stretched across the sky. They came in 'families' of about seventy planes each.

"Maybe those gigantic waves were two miles apart, maybe they were ten miles. I don't know. But I do know they came in a constant procession and I thought it would never end. What the Germans must have thought is beyond comprehension.

"The flight across the sky was slow and steady. I've never known a storm, or a machine, or any resolve of man that had about it the aura of such a ghastly restlessness. I had the feeling that had God appeared beseechingly before them in the sky, with palms outstretched to persuade them back, they would not have had within them the power to turn from that irresistible course...

"The first huge flight passed directly overhead and others followed. We spread out our feet trying to look straight up, until our steel helmets fell off... and then the bombs came! They began like a crackle of popcorn and almost instantly swelled into a monstrous fury of noise that seemed surely to destroy all the world ahead of us... the bright day grew slowly dark from it. By now everything was an indescribable caldron of sounds. Individual noises did not exist. The thundering of the motors in the sky and the roar of bombs ahead filled all the space for noise on earth. Our own heavy artillery was crashing all around us, yet we could hardly hear it.

"The Germans began to shoot heavy, high ack-ack. Great black puffs of it by the score speckled the sky, until it was hard to distinguish smoke puffs from planes. And then someone shouted that one of the planes was smoking. Yes, we could all see it. A long faint line of black smoke stretched straight for a mile behind one of them. And as we watched, there was a gigantic sweep of flame over the plane. From nose to tail it disappeared in flame, it slanted slowly down and banked around the sky in great wide curves, this way and that way, as rhythmically and gracefully as in a slow motion waltz... and then, just as slowly it turned over and dived for the earth—a golden spearhead on the straight black shaft of its own creation—and disappeared behind the treetops.

"Before it was down, there were more cries of, 'There's another one smoking and there's a third one now.' Chutes came out of some of the planes. Out of some came no chutes at all. One of white silk caught on the tail of a plane. Men with binoculars could see him fighting to get loose until flames swept over him, and then a tiny black dot fell through space, all alone.

"And all that time the great flat ceiling of the sky was roofed by all the other planes that didn't go down, plowing their way forward as if there were no turmoil in the world. They stalked on, slowly and with a dreadful pall of sound...

"God, how we admired those men up there and were sickened for the ones who fell."

Then, as we know now, the smoke markers began to drift over our own lines. As the smoke drifted back, our planes dropped bombs on our own forces. One hundred and two American soldiers were killed and 380 wounded. Ernie Pyle continues:

"It is possible to become so enthralled by some of the spectacles of war that a man is momentarily captivated away from his own danger. That's what happened to our little group of soldiers as we stood watching the mighty bombing. But that benign state didn't last long. As we watched, the exploding bombs were easing back toward us, flight by flight, instead of gradually forward as the plan called for.

"...An indescribable kind of panic came over us. We stood tensed and muscle and frozen in intellect, watching each flight approach and pass over, feeling trapped and completely helpless. And then all of an instant the universe became filled with a gigantic rattling as of huge ripe seeds in a mammoth dry gourd. I doubt that any of us had heard that sound before, but instinct told us what it was. It was bombs by the hundreds, hurtling down through the air above us.

"Many times I've heard bombs whistle or swish or rustle, but never before had I heard bombs rattle...it is an awful sound...We dived...some got into dugouts...others foxholes, ditches, and some got behind a garden wall—although which side is 'behind' was anybody's guess...I remember hitting the ground flat, all spread out like the cartoons of people flattened by steamrollers, and then squirming like an eel to get under one of the heavy wagons in the shed.

"An officer wriggled in beside me. We stopped...feeling it was hopeless to move farther...we lay with our heads slightly up—like two snakes. I know what was in both our minds and our eyes, asking each other what to do."

Ernie Pyle survived this episode and other narrow escapes in the course of his career as a combat correspondent. Then one day, on an obscure Pacific island—Ie Shima—Ernie Pyle's number finally came up. He was killed by a direct hit from a Japanese mortar in a ditch he had dived into in an attempt to survive.

His description of the bomber stream and the relentless ability of the 8th to continue with its terrible mission of destruction of the German army is one of the finest of many accounts of the "breakout" from St. Lo.

The 1919 U.S. Army Air Service Flying Regulations

From the Great Memory Book of Ed Wanner, 445th

1. Don't take the machine into the air unless you are satisfied it will fly.
2. Never leave the ground with the motor leaking.
3. Don't turn sharply when taxiing, instead of turning short, have someone lift the tail around.
4. In taking off, look at the ground and the air.
5. Never get out of a machine with the motor running until the pilot relieving you can reach the engine controls.
6. Pilots should carry hankies in a handy position to wipe off goggles.

7. Riding on the steps, wing, or tail of a machine is prohibited.

8. In case the engine fails on takeoff, land straight ahead regardless of obstacles.

9. No man must taxi faster than a man can walk.

10. Do not use altitude instruments.

11. Learn to gauge altitude, especially on landing.

12. If you see another machine near you, get out of its way.

13. No two cadets should ever ride together in the same machine.

14. Never run motor so that blast will blow on other machines.

15. Before you begin a landing glide, see that no machines are under you.

16. Hedge-hopping will not be tolerated.

17. No spins on back or tail slides will be indulged in, as they unnecessarily strain the machine.

18. If flying against the wind, and you wish to turn and fly with the wind, don't make the sharp turn near the ground. You might crash!

19. Motors have been known to stop during a long slide. If pilot wishes to use motor for landing, he should open throttle.

20. Don't attempt to force machines onto the ground with more than flying speed. The result is bouncing and ricocheting.

21. Aviators will not wear spurs while flying.

22. Do not use aeronautical gas in cars and motorcycles.

23. You must not take off or land closer than 50 feet to the hangar.

24. Never take a machine into the air until you are familiar with its controls and instruments.

25. If an emergency occurs while flying, land as soon as possible.

26. It is advisable to carry a good pair of pliers in a position where both pilot and passenger can reach them in case of an accident.

27. Joy rides will not be given to civilians.

Tales of the 44th:
Return to Keller

Forrest S. Clark

It is imperative that future generations understand the fullest possible perspective on World War II and the kind of forces that opposed each other in the war. The following is meant to give that perspective to show compassion to the victims and survivors of that terrible war. This is based on an eyewitness account of one of the 8th Air Force bombing raids and contains only the truth as it happened fifty years ago.

The air raid sirens had sounded that cold snowy November day shortly after 11 AM.

A 14 year old Norwegian schoolgirl remembered that day fifty years ago.

"I've got to get home. What's happened to my mother?" she said out loud as she rode her bike up the hill toward her home. The year was 1943, the time of the German occupation of Norway, a time of terror and fear. She had huddled in the bomb shelter while the bombs shook the earth.

Smoke was still rising all about her, and huge holes in the ground showed where the bombs had fallen, making the familiar countryside look like "a landscape of the moon." A short time before she had huddled with others of her classmates in a basement air raid shelter as the bombs fell, shaking the ground, sending dust and debris down on the children. They sang as loud as they could to overcome their fear, but they were still shivering with fright.

After school she was so anxious to find her home and her mother amid the confusion that she rode furiously in the direction of her homestead above the airfield. Fires were all about her, but she rode on and on.

She was stopped by German guards on the road to her home. They said she could not pass. They did not want anyone to pass the airfield and see the damage.

"But that's my home up there," she told the guards.

One German guard looked at her very carefully with a stern expression and asked for her identification card. He blocked her way with his gun.

She handed him her card and he looked at it for a long time. Then he turned to another officer standing nearby and said, "Wait."

It was at that time she noted that there was a huge car with flags on it and several officers standing about it. This car was obviously a command car for a German high-ranking officer. Little did she know that Gen. von Falkenhorst, commander of German forces in Norway, was there that day observing a military exercise of the troops.

In a little while the guard came back and said, "Pass." Out of a corner of one eye the girl saw the officers train their field glasses down on the airfield where huge fires were burning.

Later she was to discover that 29 big bombs had landed around her home and seven unexploded bombs were still buried. But the house was not hit.

"It was as if somebody had held an umbrella above our

house," she said. That somebody must have been God, she admitted years later.

Gen. von Falkenhorst had recently received orders from no less than the German High Command and Hitler to increase security and defense readiness around the Norwegian bases. This was the result of the very recent commando raids and bombing missions against Nazi-occupied Norway. Two days before the Kjeller bomb raid, Allied bombers had struck a blow at the highly important secret operations on Rjukan where heavy water was being processed for experimentation for the atomic bomb. This raid had incensed the German commanders, and word had gone forth to prevent such a surprise attack again.

Here two days later at Kjeller when the first U.S. bombers appeared, the German officers assured Gen. von Falkenhorst that they were friendly aircraft taking part in the military exercise. However, a tremendous salvo of bombs set off from a few hundred yards downhill from the general's position sent all officers running for cover. The general observed all this and did not have much time to pay attention to the small teenage girl asking permission to proceed up the road to her farmhouse.

The impact of the bombs was particularly frightening because most of Kjeller and the nearby village of Lillestrøm were under laid with peat, a substance of jelly-like properties that accentuated the vibrations and prolonged them.

The Norwegians thought they had been forgotten by the Allies and the U.S. Air Force because they had not seen any bombers over their town, only Germans since April of 1940, the date of the German invasion of Norway. Some Norwegians on that November day in 1943 ran outside in the snow and waved at the American bombers. One Norwegian mother shouted, "Those are my boys up there."

The bombing destroyed 85% of the airfield facilities, crippling a major repair depot and German base.

Fifty years later the Americans who bombed the base returned, this time for a friendly reception by the people. Among them was that once teenage girl who had been so frightened and terrorized by the bombing and the German officers.

She is now a mature woman, Sidsel Brun, whose father was commander-in-chief of the Kjeller base before the German occupation. He was a prisoner of war in Germany for nearly the entire war, and returned by some miracle to survive and join his family. Her mother was a prominent woman in Norway, a singer of note and well-liked by the people.

This is merely one of the many stories of the survivors of that fearful time, a time when courage was a daily part of living. Courage was also the price of survival.

There is a new American memorial at Kjeller to airmen and Norwegians who lost their lives in World War II. It was dedicated on the 50th anniversary of the Kjeller mission by survivors of that mission. The memorial is a small part of America in the middle of Norway and the Norwegians have promised to honor it and protect it forever.

Norway Remembers
Americans' Sacrifice
Ed Dobson, Jr. AM, 44th BG

Lt. Ed Dobson was one of many young men who answered the call to fight in World War II. And like too many others, Lt. Dobson did not come home. After his commissioning as a combat pilot in the Army Air Force, Lt. Dobson served and gave his life in a four engine B-24 Liberator bomber. On May 8, 1995, commemorating the 50th anniversary of the end of the war in Europe, Norwegians dedicated a stone monument with bronze plaque to Lt. Dobson and 62 other American fliers who lost their lives on the mission that began the liberation of Norway.

Lt. Dobson's last mission took him to Norway on November 18, 1943. On the 50th anniversary of that mission in 1993, several men who flew the mission gathered in Norway as guests of the Royal Norwegian Air Force. Over 400 Norwegians filled a church at Lillestrom for the commemorative service. Many had been tortured during the war as members of the resistance.

Lt. Dobson had been assigned to the 8th Air Force as copilot on the crew of Lt. James E. Hill of Midland, TX. They were sent to the 67th Squadron of the 44th Bomb Group, stationed in England, as a replacement crew.

The 67th Squadron was suffering terrible losses, being mathematically entirely wiped out twice by the fall of 1943. On two missions, August 16 and October 1, 1943, while the 67th was on temporary duty based in North Africa, Lt. Dobson's B-24 was the only plane of the squadron that got to the target and returned to base. In October 1943 the remnants of the 67th returned to England. There, Lt. Dobson accomplished the goal of all copilots; promotion to first pilot with his own plane and crew.

Lt. Dobson knew his job, and he knew the odds. At that time in the war, combat crews had to fly 25 missions. The top brass adopted that number based on an expected 4% loss rate per mission. There was some talk of lowering the requirement to 15 missions, but that never happened. The men figured their life expectancy at eight missions. After eight, they figured they were living on borrowed time.

Until the morning of November 16, 1943, when the mission officer first lifted the curtain from the map to expose a target in Norway, none of the B-24 crews in England expected to go there. The trip involved 1400 miles, mostly over the frigid North Sea. A parachute was only short-term help and rescue virtually impossible. But the Germans had a heavy water plant in Norway, a key to their effort to be first with the atomic bomb.

On November 16th, four bomb groups, the 44th, 93rd, 389th, and 392nd, were assigned to the heavy water target. The weather did not cooperate. Most planes, including Lt. Dobson's, were called back. Planes that arrived in Norway could not find the heavy water plant, but a vital chemical plant was destroyed. There was little flak, no enemy aircraft, and no American losses. Later, the heavy water plant and its product were disabled and destroyed by

Norwegians on the ground, led by the late Knut Haukelid and now known as the Heroes of Telemark.

On November 18, when the curtain went up to reveal Norway again, the men were more concerned about the long flight over cold weather than about enemy opposition. This time the target was a German fighter repair base outside Oslo. Joseph Stalin was demanding that the Allies open a campaign on the western front to divert Hitler's attention from Russia. D-Day was still half a year away. The Germans' fighter repair base outside Oslo was servicing their fighters from the Russian front. Our bombers would answer Stalin's demands.

One hundred and seven planes of the same four bomb groups lifted from their bases in the dark of that fogbound and icy morning. In a portent of what was to happen, the 44th was unable to accomplish its formation assembly. Tail-end planes starting late for Norway expected to assemble on the way. Because of this, when the German fighters did come, it was difficult for American flyers to identify their own damaged aircraft.

And come the Germans did. Fighters based in Denmark intercepted the tail of the formation going in, and most of the formation going back, especially the "tail-end Charlies." Lt. Dobson and the rest of the 44th were "tail-end Charlies" that day.

Of the 107 crews from the four groups, three landed in neutral Sweden without loss of life. Only six of the 107 crews were lost. Of those six, four were 44th "Flying Eight-Ball" crews. Three of the four were 67th Squadron crews, and the fourth pilot, Lt. Ed Mitchell, was an original 67th Squadron pilot who had just transferred to another squadron. The 67th's bad luck had struck again.

A report shows that Lt. Dobson made the bomb run and dropped on target, but no one knows what happened to

Lt. Dobson and his crew. Two B-24s were positively identified going down in the North Sea on the return, but neither plane was Dobson's. That left two 67th planes unaccounted for and declared missing in action.

One of those two was piloted by Lt. Earl Johnson of Montgomery, Alabama. One 67th crew was reported shot down in the Skagerrak, the sea south of Oslo, prior to the bomb run. That plane must have been Lt. Johnson's. At the end of the war, both crews were declared killed in action. Lt. Dobson is presumed shot down over the North Sea.

The mission was termed a success, as over 70% of our bombs fell within 2,000 feet of the briefed aiming point. Working with the Norwegian Resistance, the Air Force picked a day when the Norwegian work force was on holiday. Only three Norwegians died in the raid. Two half-sisters attending the 50th anniversary in 1993 had lost their father, and one had lost her mother. The two sisters were teens that day, schoolgirls huddled in a bomb shelter.

Later, both women said that they never blamed the Americans for their personal losses that day. They always thought of the Nazis as ultimately responsible for those events.

One of the sisters, Lil Nyheim, invited the Americans to her house the next day for waffles, a traditional Norwegian hospitality meal. On the wall of her living room was a large and beautiful painting with a hole in it. She explained that the hole had been made by a bomb fragment, probably the bomb that killed her parents. Her parents were trying to get away from their house close to the airfield, perhaps thinking that they would be safer in the woods. They suffered a direct hit and died instantly.

Afterwards, as the small party of Americans gathered in their large van, expressing thanks and love to Lil Nyheim, she waved her goodbye with a four-foot Norwegian flag. Lil and other Norwegians are serious about remembering the American airmen who came to help liberate Norway some fifty years ago, especially those like Lt. Ed Dobson who gave their lives. The permanent stone and bronze memorial was dedicated on May 8th at the air base that was their target that day more than fifty years ago. It is a monument to Norwegian-American friendship as well as to the 63 American fliers and three Norwegians lost that day.

In Lt. Ed Dobson's hometown of Merrick, New York, Dobson Avenue is a reminder of his courage and commitment.

Incident On Kiel
Mission - B17 - 96th
BG

The following comments regarding a mission to Kiel were printed in the June, 1984 Second Air Division Journal Association's *The Journal*, its official publication. In that I have misplaced that issue, only Roger Freeman's comments are presented here. In researching for the mission in Mr. Freeman's *Mighty Eighth War Diary* I'm quite certain this was a 14 May 1943 mission flown by five B-17 groups and the one B-24 group, the 44th. The toll was the loss of eight bombers, 5-24s and 3-17s, 36 damaged, three killed in action, seventeen wounded, and eighty-one missing, per Freeman. He included an addendum entitled "INCIDENT," partially, as follows:

One bomber was lost through an unusual accident. Shortly after takeoff a B-17 was critically damaged by a run-away machine gun. The weapon was in the left waist internally stowed and was being checked by the gunner when accidentally discharged.

Bullets went through the side of the fuselage and shot away half the right horizontal stabilizer and severed the control cables on that side of the bomber. The waist gunner was injured and the tail gunner seriously wounded by the burst. Pilot, Capt. Derrol Rogers, managed to keep control but found he could only fly the aircraft in a gradual turn. Coming back to the vicinity of the base, the wounded tail gunner and the other five men in the rear of the bomber were ordered to bail out, after which Rogers continued in a wide circle towards the Wash and the bombs were jettisoned. Believing that the damage to the aircraft would make a safe landing impossible, Rogers had the bombardier and navigator parachute, and when the orbit brought the bomber back over the Wash he and the copilot followed. It was an hour and a half before 2nd Lt. Norville Gorse, the copilot, by then suffering from exposure, was found and rescued from the water. The search continued for Rogers and when eventually located, he was dead. This tragic accident brought a directive that in future, guns were not to be adjusted or primed while in the stowed position.

Princess' Death Ends Fairy Tale

Thrity Umrigar

Akron Beacon Journal, August 2, 1993

The princess died in Bucharest, Romania, in May. In Tallmadge, Ohio, a 75 year old man was overcome with grief. He wasn't the only one. For Clell Riffle and many of the men who served with him in World War II, it was the end of an era.

Princess Catherine Caradja's death may have marked the symbolic end of the most painful period of Riffle's life. But it did not—could not—mark the end of a friendship that began in a cornfield in Brasov/Ploesti, Romania, in 1943.

On August 1, 1943, Riffle was one of the 560 men sent by the U.S. Air Force to bomb the oil fields of Ploesti. Only 110 of the men survived the attack and Riffle was one of them—thanks to the courage of a Romanian princess with a heart of gold.

After they had successfully bombed some of Ploesti's oil refineries, Riffle's plane was shot down. The injured men crash-landed in a cornfield. Riffle himself was hit in the knees and had broken ribs. But his worst nightmare was yet to come.

Within minutes, the cornfields parted and Riffle and his

comrades were greeted by German and Romanian soldiers. A German officer, not realizing that Riffle was injured, ordered him to get up. As Riffle looked helplessly on, the officer picked up a hand grenade and aimed it at him.

Just then, a handsome, distinguished looking woman strode onto the scene. "Who are you?" she asked the visitors.

"We're Americans."

She turned to the German officer and fixed an imperial gaze upon him. Slowly, the hand holding the grenade lowered.

The fifty-something woman turned out to be Princess Caradja. The cornfield was part of her estate. And although she was limited in what she could do for her American "boys," she continued to help them.

Riffle remembers the first time the princess visited them in the Romanian POW camp he was detained in for 13 months. "I cried," he recalls. Then, he cries again, as if it were 1943 instead of 1993.

The princess would smuggle in wire cutters, glue and other tools to help the Americans escape. When they would thank her, she'd reply, "My dear, I do what I can."

Riffle never got a chance to thank the princess again until 1955. By then, the tables had turned. This time, she was a visitor to his country and it was her fortunes that had come tumbling down. The Communist regime in Romania had stripped her of most of her wealth and she feared for her life. She escaped from her homeland, smuggled out on a vehicle carrying refrigerator coils.

When Riffle spotted the princess on a television talk show in America, he could not believe his eyes. He contacted her and four months later, she came to visit the home of one of her boys. For the rest of her life, whenever she wanted a break from the lecture circuit she embarked upon in America, she would visit the Tallmadge home.

Until 1991. With Romania free from its dictatorship, the princess wanted to return to the homeland she had never forgotten.

"My dear," she had once told Riffle, "once these bones are finished, I hope they're buried in Romania to fertilize those beautiful plains."

And now it has come to pass. Princess Catherine Caradja died on May 26 in the Bucharest orphanage she had founded decades ago. She was 100.

Riffle says if he could talk to his beloved princess once more, he'd say: "For what you've contributed to mankind, to the true values that each human must love, I salute you."

Then he falls silent. But his teary eyes write the final eulogy for the aristocrat who had the heart of a lion.

Author's note: Clell Riffle was a radio operator aboard the 389th's "Chattanooga Choo Choo" on the August 1, 1943 Ploesti mission.

The Revenge of
Corporal Weinberg

Lt. Samuel W. Taylor, HQ. USSTAF

Reprinted from the Sept. 1945 issue of Air Force Magazine
When, in November of 1938, the Gestapo threw a 16 year old boy into a concentration camp, they didn't dream of the retribution it would entail. He was but one of thousands of boys taken in a roundup following the death of a member of the German legation in Paris named Von Rath who was allegedly killed by a young Jewish boy. The Nazis might well regret that. Despite the brutal treatment they received, he and his family managed to get to America, where Erwin eventually became a corporal in the U.S. Army Air Force.

Corporal Weinberg was never to fly a mission, drop a bomb, or fire a .50 caliber machine gun at the enemy. Yet he was to enlist the enormous might of the 8th Air Force to settle his personal score. He had a very large account to settle with the Gestapo, and now that his people would not suffer any more, his story can be told.

He and his father were arrested and thrown into a boxcar crammed with other Jews. They knew their destination was

Buchenwald, a name to be spoken in a whisper even in 1938. At Weimar, they were ordered out, faced against a wall and beaten over the head from behind with rubber truncheons by SS troopers.

"This wasn't the experimentation program," Erwin Weinberg said. "That didn't come until later. The Nazis merely wanted to discourage us and get us out of Germany. We were to be released if we could arrange to get out of the country." Experimentation or not, five hundred Jews died the first month.

The Weinberg family had been trying to get to America since 1936 and their names reached the top of the waiting list in 1940. Erwin arrived in his new country on a Tuesday and went to work Friday morning in a Philadelphia factory making Army uniforms, where he sewed GI blouses and waited.

The British began bombing Germany after they won the Battle of Britain and from that Erwin got the idea of how to settle the score. But he was just one person and he didn't know how to go about doing what he wanted to do. When America entered the war, he couldn't enlist because he was an alien. He wondered whom he could tell his idea to, but it seemed impossible that anyone would listen.

There is something about determination that makes the breaks. He earned his citizenship papers after taking classes at night and that helped a lot.

In June 1943, the Army accepted him for the Air Force and that was just where he wanted to be. The following February he landed in England, again just where he wanted to be. But still, he was only a private at the very bottom of Army channels. What could a lowly private do to convince the Army brass that he had a good idea?

He obtained permission from his 1st Sergeant to speak to an officer. "Sir, I have information that I think is of value to the 8th Air Force. My hometown is Fulda, Germany. Fulda has never been bombed, yet there is a ball bearing factory there, Gebauer and Moller. Gummiwerke Fulda AG is a rubber factory and there is also an enamel factory making war materials. I know the location of all three plants."

The officer listened and suggested that Erwin talk to an intelligence officer. Two days later Pvt. Weinberg was transferred to the U.S. Strategic Air Forces in Europe where he talked with a Major John Simone. Major Simone was more than interested. He called for the target folder on Fulda and learned that a ball bearing plant was known to be there, but its location was unknown. Intelligence was not sure which of the two factories was the rubber plant.

To prove he knew what he was talking about, Weinberg took pencil and paper and drew a sketch showing the two plants in relation to roads and rivers. Satisfied, the major requested air reconnaissance on the target, but the air forces were very busy, at the time, preparing for D-Day and other reconnaissance targets had priority over Fulda.

Erwin was then assigned the job of interpreter and file clerk for reconnaissance photos. As each new batch of photos came in, he hoped one of them would be Fulda. Meanwhile, the attacks on ball bearing plants were discontinued—their purpose of impairing the production of ordnance and aircraft had been achieved. Aren't they ever going to bomb Fulda?

Then one day the major called him in and handed him several reconnaissance photos of Fulda. "Can you pinpoint these three targets?" "Yes Sir, I sure can!" And Private Weinberg proceeded to circle the ball bearing plant, the rubber factory and the factory that had been making enamel.

Finally, in August, the major called him in again and showed him a series of strike photos of bombs exploding on the rubber plant and in the marshaling yards. A photo taken after reconnaissance showed extensive damage to both.

Eighth Air Force heavy bombers struck Fulda twice more in December 1944, again in January 1945 and again in March. To make sure the three plants were completely destroyed, the 9th Air Force sent medium bombers to hit the target one last time in April.

Weinberg's targets were bombed six times on the basis of information he had supplied and he began to collect spare photos of them. The one he likes most of all shows where a bomb fell outside the target area and made a direct hit on his father's house. This was one of the houses the Nazis took without payment. Now they would never be able to use it.

Private Erwin was a little disappointed in the fact that they never sent a lot of bombers over Fulda, never more than 100 in any one raid. However, even that was a pretty fair sized air force for a lowly private. "I think I did all I could for the 8th Air Force," he said.

He is now a corporal, but he doesn't connect his promotion to his contribution towards the destruction of the Fulda target. He says it's just Army T/O.

His one remaining goal is to visit Fulda, after the war, to view the destruction. Considering what he accomplished as a private, no one doubts that he will be able to do just that.

We are the Mustangs, Your "Little Friends" of World War II!

Robert E. Kuhnert, 355th FG

The 355th Fighter Group has a rich heritage, being descended from perhaps the most illustrious pursuit group in the annals of aerial warfare—the legendary 1st Pursuit Group of World War I, which flew Nieuport 28s, Spads and Sopwith Camels. Capt. Eddie Rickenbacker, America's "ace of aces in WWI," was commanding officer of the 94th (hat-in-ring) Squadron.

In our World War II days we thought of those flimsy WWI fabric-and-wood flying machines as "crates" compared with our mighty all-metal P-47 Thunderbolt and the long-range, highly maneuverable P-51 Mustang, both heavily armed with terrifying multiple 50 caliber machine guns (which fired outside the arc of the propeller). And now our "superior" airplanes seem almost antiquated in the eyes of our young as they watch on TV, sitting in easy chairs at home, present-day jet fighters sending electronically controlled weapons into doorways with surgical precision.

I recall the influx of brand new "gold bar second looies" with shiny silver sings, some of whom commanded 355th Fighter Squadrons and became excellent combat pilots, many of them aces. Sadly, some of them fell in combat and became prisoners of war; too many paid the supreme price of life; happily, some evaded capture and returned. It is a gratifying feeling (as one ages) to remember helping "wet-nurse" those young men who distinguished themselves in combat.

The 355th Fighter Group led all fighter groups in the 8th Air Force in the dangerous role of ground strafing, earning the title "Steeple Morden Strafers." Our group emerged from the war in either third or fourth place in combined air/ground victories. There may be a discrepancy in placement. I like to use information released by the 8th Air Force, and printed in the war-time newspaper *Stars and Stripes*. An article from S&S in my scrapbook lists the 355th in third place, showing 356 destroyed in the air, and 504 on the ground, a total of 860; the 355th bested only by the longer-serving 4th Fighter Group (formerly the Eagle Squadrons), and Lt. Col. "Gabby" Gabreski's much-touted 6th Fighter Group.

The 355th can boast having, at one time, the ETO's leading ace, as reported in another *Stars and Stripes* article. Capt. (now retired Colonel) Henry Brown, 354th FS, was the high scorer when Lt. Col. Gabreski went down, Henry having a combined total of 30. He needed only one more to tie Gabreski's record. As fate would have it, we lost our top ace, Henry Brown, to ground fire and POW status. We have him back and have enjoyed him at reunions.

Memorable events are chronicled in the history of our 355th. On April 5, 1944, shortly after switching from P-47s to P-51s, the 355th made a daring and dangerous—and profitable—raid on a German airfield in a raging snowstorm. For that mission the group was awarded the Distinguished Unit Citation (which is often referred to, and is currently listed in *Air Force Magazine* as, the Presidential Unit Citation).

There are interesting, exciting cliff-hanging stories which could fill a book, and there is a book which reviews and relates all missions and events. For those who may not yet be familiar with it, Bill Marshall (son of the late Col. Bert Marshall, one-time C.O. of the 354th FS) has written and published an excellent history of the 355th in WWII. Its appropriate title is *Angels, Bulldogs & Dragons* (nicknames of the three squadrons). We've distributed about 200 copies to members and friends through our 355th PX, and it is available in many bookstores, particularly in the air museums.

A first in WWII was achieved by 355th pilots: the daring "piggyback" rescue of Bert Marshall behind enemy lines by Royce Priest (now a retired Colonel), both returning to Steeple Morden in Priest's P-51. That story received wide publicity, and is told in *Angels, Bulldogs & Dragons*. That morale-building snatch-from-the-jaws-of-capture retrieval took place on August 18, 1944, just a couple hours prior to another fine morale-building event: the great Glenn Miller concert in our Steeple Morden airfield hangar.

Ken Williams (354th FS in WWII, now a retired Lt. Col.) was our 355th pilot to go down in France (26 March 1944), evade and return to Steeple Morden in a very few weeks. Bill Cullerton may well be the only pilot known to survive a bullet from his own .45 going all the way through his body, then to escape, evade, and meet up with friendly forces.

We believe Bill Cullerton (357th FS) was the first pilot in the ETO to destroy eight enemy airplanes in one day. First ace in the 2nd Scouting Force (whose primary mission was not fighting) was Bill Whalen. The 2nd Scouting Force operated out of Steeple Morden airdrome, was supported by the 355th, and is an integral part of our 355th story today).

The second ace of WWII was Carrol McColpin (355th HQ, now retired Major General). He had served with RAF Eagle SQ 133 and the 4th Fighter Group before joining the 355th. Aces-in-a-day (combining both air and ground totals): Henry Brown, Bill Cullerton, John "Moon" Elder, Billy Hovde, Claiborne Kinnard, Halbert Marsh, Jim McElroy, Joe Mellen, Duran Vickery, Bob Woody, and Bob Peters.

Six 355th pilots destroyed the new, mysterious and dreaded ME-262 German jet fighter: Charles Spencer, 354th FS; Wendell Beatty, 358th FS; John Wilkins, 2SF; Charles Redenbaugh, 2SF, and Elmer Riffle, 357th FS. Henry Kirby, 357th FS, shared an ME-262, and Gene Greenwell, 2SF, damaged one.

The 355th flew the last England-Russia-Italy-England shuttle mission, escorting bombers on a mercy mission on 18 September 1944 to drop supplies to beleaguered Polish forces at Warsaw, continuing on to Russia for a refueling stop, then on to Italy and back to England on 22 September.

We cite one more instance of bravery, above and beyond, by ground personnel when, on 1 January 1945, a B-17 from Bassingbourn (91st Bomb Group) crashed on our airdrome, killing all aboard. It destroyed one P-51, damaged several others, and seriously wounded crew chief Bob Marzo (354th FS). C-Flight Chief T/Sgt. Ray Katzensky and crew chief S/Sgt. Morton Braun risked their lives to save Bob Marzo by quickly removing him from the area to the base hospital. Both Ray and Mort were awarded the Soldier's Medal (highest non-combat award) for their bravery and quick action).

All the foregoing is but a "sampler" of 355th "right stuff" quality in bravery, guts, skill, honor, and duty. We can all be proud to have served in the World War II 355th Fighter Group, and to pass on this legacy to our children and grandchildren.

California, One-Way!

Ralph Elliott, 467th

It's April 29, 1993, and forty-eight years have passed since I landed my B-24 Liberator bomber, 591, at Bradley Field, Connecticut after a seven-day flight from England at the close of World War II. Unbelievably, I am again sitting in the pilot's seat, flying the last combat-ready B-24 in existence on a four-hour flight from Tucson, Arizona to Santa Monica, California. Slowly, the old skills come back, the altitude settles down on 5000 feet, and the compass heading stays on 270 degrees. Was it always this much work? No power steering here—just the cables from the controls out to the ailerons and back to the elevator and rudders. Trim tabs help to take some of the pressure off the wheel; but then reality sets in—it really was work. I just didn't know it then. The physical difference is in the age, 23 versus 71, but age has done nothing to diminish the thrill of flying the Liberator again.

Only, did they downsize her when she was rebuilt? The catwalk through the bomb bay seems narrower now, and surely four men and all their gear didn't share this little space in the rear with the guns, the flak jackets, the Mae Wests, the parachutes and sand bags. No wonder the bombardier, navigator, and nose turret gunner had a constant fight for room up front, and five men couldn't possibly fit on the flight deck. Even the pilot's seat seems smaller. What does come back are the noise of the engines that make normal conversation impossible, the smell of high-octane gasoline, and the feeling in the pit of the stomach that goes with an air pocket and a "rapid change of altitude."

The desert air is rough at low altitude and the thermals catch me as we go over a low mountain ridge into California. The other two passengers get airsick, and I'm glad I'm doing the flying—not bouncing around in the back. It's drafty back there with the side windows open for the guns, and it was hell for the gunners at 45 below zero, when to touch the guns without gloves meant you'd lose your fingers. Memories ride with me on the flight, and the years fall off in the sights and sounds and smells, but I finally realize that the real wonder is the set of circumstances that have put me up here again after an absence of 48 years.

On April 27, the "All American" arrived at the Avra Valley Airport, north of Tucson, on a cross-country tour sponsored by the College (isn't it Collins?) Foundation of Stow, Massachusetts. During WWII, the B-24 dropped more bombs and flew more missions than any other aircraft; it was the most produced aircraft of all time—over 18,000 planes. The cost to reconstruct the "All American" was over $1,300,000.00, but money can't buy the feelings of nostalgia and the tears the old bomber generates as the veterans stand on the ramp and cheer as she taxis in.

Unbeknownst to me, as a 50th wedding anniversary present (August 28), Yvonne had contacted the organizers of the Avra Valley stop and had made arrangements for me to fly in the plane on the next leg of her flight to California. While the kids joke about "Mom giving Dad a one-way ticket to California for an anniversary present," they were as thrilled as I was about the flight. No surprise in our 50 years together ever topped this one.

France to England in

a Life Raft

Harold Benvenuti, 448th

April 1, 1944 was both my 13th mission and my lucky day. Passing over the French coast on our way to the target we lost our first engine from flak. While making our bomb run, another engine was knocked out. Leaving the target, our third engine ceased to function.

The pilot, Lt. Jack Black, (our plane was named 'Black's Widow') decided to go on as long as he could, knowing that eventually we would have to ditch. We all agreed that ditching was better than a P.O.W. camp for the remainder of the war.

As 'Black's Widow' settled toward the water, we threw out everything that wasn't nailed down, including both waist guns.

The order to prepare to ditch finally came. When we hit the water the ball turret dropped out and water came rushing in. It picked me up and whipped me against the right waist window. Dick Campbell and Wilfred Haschke went out the left waist window and I followed.

When we got to the left wing, the rubber boats were out. I got in one with Dick Campbell, Lt. Burkhartsmeir and Tex Dweaczyk.

Lt. Jack Black, Wilfred Haschke, Charles Nissen, Mike Curran and Pete Wermert were in the other. We never did see Joe Pompret, the copilot. We moved away from the plane waiting for it to go under. To our amazement the plane floated for an hour before pointing her nose down, her tail up and going under. When she was gone, we buried Charles Nissen who had died in our arms from serious injuries.

Being only ten miles off the French Coast (Dunkirk), it was logical to go there and give ourselves up. It was sixty miles to England. We took a vote and paddling to England won. Having made this decision, we checked the rafts for survival equipment. Nothing. There wasn't a thing! The only things we had were a few chocolate bars and a couple of compasses. So be it. We set our heading and paddled.

That night the water was really rough, and even though we used a couple of the parachutes to protect us from the wind, everybody was soaked and cold. We could hear planes flying overhead, but without a flashlight there was nothing we could do. Just wish them luck if they were ours and hope they didn't spot us if they were German.

Dawn broke with an overcast sky and all we could see was water in every direction. Lacking food and water we tried not to think about eating. We just continued to scan the water hoping to see land or some boats. After a few hours we did see an object coming toward us, and the closer it got the faster it seemed to be going. It turned out to be one of those buoys with food and a radio inside. I wanted to make a swim for it but I was over-ruled. The current was very fast and it went by us, or we it, before we knew it. It would have been impossible to swim against that current.

As the day went on, we heard airplane motors, but we never saw them as it was still overcast. Night came again with the water still rough and all of us wet and cold. As the night wore on we heard airplane engines, but this time we also saw anti-aircraft flashes and heard bombs exploding. We knew then that we were nearing land.

As it began to get light, a few minesweepers crossed our path off in the distance. We waved but they did not see us. By this time, we were certain that the land we were heading towards was England and we began to paddle faster. Finally, we came close to some fishing boats and started to yell and wave our arms. It first appeared that they didn't see us either and some of us started cussing as loud as we could.

Suddenly one fishing boat headed our way. The name of the boat was "The Three Brothers," and the crew quickly hauled us aboard. Another boat came along and was sent to shore to notify the authorities. The Captain of our boat told us that we were seen but they thought we were Germans. It wasn't until they heard our cussing that they knew we were "Yanks'.

We came ashore in Folkestone, and as soon as we landed, Tex went to his knees and kissed the good old English soil! A waiting ambulance took us to the Folkestone hospital. I was never so glad to get into a bed again and I have no idea how long we slept.

A few days later our new Colonel, Col. Mason, came to see us and told us that a base ambulance would be coming to pick us up. I kind of hated to leave that hospital as they were all so great to us, but it was good to get back to the base again and see familiar faces.

The Mighty Eighth Air Force Heritage Museum in Pooler, Georgia

Savannah sparks emotions that surprise you with their intensity. In an era when many view World War II as ancient history and its veterans as relics, this museum brings the hell and the heart of it up-close and very personal, reviving the sheer awe inspired by those who stared down peril in the name of freedom. Activated in Savannah in 1942 and conceived to strike a lethal blow against the Third Reich, the Mighty Eighth Air Force relentlessly bombed strategic German targets in occupied Europe ultimately capable of deploying 2,000 planes every day. Of an estimated 200,000 aviators and crewmen who flew the Eighth, 28,000 became prisoners of war, and 26,000 lost their lives. No other military command suffered a higher percentage of deaths, but not one mission was turned back by the Nazis.

On display among the exhibits are the belongings of pilots, including fleece-lined jackets emblazoned with morale-boosting artwork, and bailout kits containing compasses and syringes for morphine. The Wall of Aces is devoted to the flyers who shot down five or more enemy aircraft. In another section is a replica of the grim interior of a German POW barracks. A nearby video spotlights survivors of a POW camp as a recount their plight. Several images depict the resolve that defined the British during those bleak years.

But the museum's most spellbinding feature is the Mission Experience Theater, which, with authentic film footage, puts you in the center of a bombing raid. Eight screens are filled with terrifying, exhilarating action punctuated by the deafening sounds of air combat. You are there in the aircraft dodging bursts of flak and barreling assaults of the German Luftwaffe, the heavens raining parachutes and airplane fragments. Ultimately locating your target, you drop your explosive payload. At the moment that the bomb bay opens, a whoosh of air sweeps into the theater—a special effect that struck a resounding chord with 1996 visitor Walter Cronkite, who flew with the Eighth as a war correspondent.

Shot Down by the Battleship Archangel

Earl Zimmerman, 389th

I enjoyed Ken Driscoll's article about the black Libs flying out of Harrington, as I know whereof he writes. I was flying out of Leuchars, Scotland during that time and know the details of the black Lib that was shot down by the Russians near Murmansk. One of the gunners on that crew was from my original crew of the 389th, Lt. Harold L. James, pilot.

The black Libs flying out of Leuchars were assigned to the Ball Project, with Colonel Bernt Balchen as commander. He wore the Medal of Honor and the crews really liked him. I had the privilege of flying with him on two occasions.

On 20 September 1944, Colonel Keith Allen, pilot; Captain Schreiner, copilot; and seven crew members took off from Leuchars on an operational mission to drop supplies to the underground in Norway. After crossing the coastline of Norway, number one engine began to smoke and run rough. This condition existed until they reached the target area and released the containers. The engine then caught fire and was feathered, and the fire extinguished itself. After a short staff meeting on the flight deck it was decided to try for Murmansk, as heading back over the North Sea on three engines was a bit risky.

The plane finally crossed the mouth of Kola inlet as the crew looked for a place to land. Three searchlight cones of three each were turned on, indicating an airfield. In attempting to make a 360 turn, without knowing it the pilot flew over the battleship *Archangel*. During this time, the Russian colors of the day were being fired from the Very pistol; all lights on the plane were turned on, including the landing lights; and calls were being made on the International Distress Frequency.

At this time, the battleship *Archangel* opened fire along with some shore batteries, hitting engine number two which caught fire, shooting off the left rudder and damaging the left wing. With the plane on fire, Col. Allen ordered Capt. Schreiner to bail out the crew, advising that he would follow. Despite the flames, the engineer released two life rafts through the bomb bay. The right waist gunner was hit by flak and bailed out; the navigator escaped through the nose wheel well after destroying all the classified material and making sure the IFF was destroyed.

When his parachute deployed, the navigator looked up and saw his plane explode. When he reached the ground, he threw his gun away and called for the other crew members. His call was answered by machine gun fire. Eventually, he was captured by a Russian lieutenant who took him before Russian engineers for questioning, after which they were convinced of his identity. A Russian staff officer took him to view the plane, which was entirely demolished, and on his return to the Russian quarters he identified the remains of Colonel Allen.

The Russians relinquished control of the crew to Captain S. B. Frankel, USN, who dispatched a message to London. Burial rites for Colonel Allen were conducted by Captain Frankel, in the presence of Russian Admiral Golovko, Commander Morton, Royal

Navy and local diplomatic agents, with six of the ambulatory crew members acting as pallbearers. A farewell salute was fired by a Russian Guard of Honor.

All crew members were happy to get out from under the jurisdiction of the Russians as they boarded the HMS Rodney, which took them to the naval air station at Scapa Flow where they disembarked. Two amphibious aircraft took the crew back to the home base at Leuchars, Scotland.

RAF Leuchars was a strange airfield. Among other units stationed there were the Green Libs, Operation "Sonnie," with civilian markings, flying into Sweden bringing out the American internees; a Canadian outfit flying white Libs on sub patrol; Royal Navy fabric covered biplanes, fitted with torpedoes; strange looking aircraft which were crewed by French, Polish, Norwegians and South Africans, and a few assorted uniforms which could not be distinguished. Our operation was restricted to a small area around a hangar, and we met the other crews at the local pubs but none would reveal their missions.

The Carpetbaggers had missions to Norway, Denmark, Holland, Belgium, Germany and France. Some crews, dressed in civilian clothing, flew across Norway and landed in neutral Sweden to drop off or pick up VIPs. Major William E. Colby, who in later years became director of our Central Intelligence Agency (CIA), was dropped by a Carpetbagger aircraft in France during August 1944 and dropped again in Norway about March, 1945.

In mid-1944, the Carpetbaggers only flew black B-24 type aircraft. As the months went on, they had a few C-47s that they flew and landed behind enemy lines in France. They also flew some modified A-26 aircraft and British Mosquitos to drop agents deep in Germany.

An incident happened one night at Harrington that I have never forgotten. We had been briefed in the afternoon that our drop site was in Belgium and that we would be dropping two agents. As a general rule, air crews did not mingle with the agents to be dropped. I, as pilot, usually introduced myself to them, time permitting, and asked if they had any questions about the flight or drop.

As I approached the two agents, who were standing near the nose of the aircraft just prior to boarding, I noted that one of them was a lady about 20-25 years old. Just before I got to them, I saw their escort hand them some capsules. These capsules contained poison and were to be swallowed by the agents to kill themselves, if they so desired, when they were captured. If captured, they would have been tortured as spies and put to death by the Germans. Seeing this young lady voluntarily embark on such a dangerous mission, knowing the consequences if it failed, has been etched in my memory ever since.

Midnight

by the author

The door opens in our heavily black-out-curtained concrete barracks. Home to a dozen flying officers—three each pilots, copilots, navigators, bombardiers. "BRIEFING AT ONE" is the unwelcome message. The gut recoils at the prospect of the day. The place is near the city of Norwich, capital of East Anglia, in east central England. It's at U.S. Army Air Forces' B-24 base. I both roll and stumble out of my army cot, along with the three other officers in my crew—along with any other crews who may have been assigned to this mission. We trudge, heavily booted, in the dark to the lavatory. We shave closely in order to get a close fit on our oxygen masks. Then a couple of blocks to the mess where we are often served fresh eggs, but they have been barely warmed in the pan, and the worried stomach can't face them. We know that a couple of cups of coffee, along with the adrenaline we'll muster, will carry us through the next ten hours. We either catch a truck or ride our bikes to operations, and the four officers join the six enlisted men of our crew. We don't feel like a small army, but we are. We're not mad at anybody, but we believe we are preserving our world of freedom of choice and absence of fear, which we wouldn't be if we lose. While we are concerned about winning, we are possessed with survival. A mission is personally successful primarily if we get back safely, and secondarily, if we destroyed our target. Not that it wasn't important. If you didn't, a return trip would be necessary. And you are never more alive than after escaping the alternative. After the general briefing, the noncoms go to our assigned plane to prepare for the flight. The pilots go to a separate briefing room, and the navigator and bombardier to another. Here, intricate details of the flight are covered. It's a big job to put up a thousand or more airplanes in the sky—every day—get them organized and on their way to maybe a dozen or more targets, and coordinate fighter protection. It's a ready-made situation for foul ups, and they occur with regularity.

After these briefings the officers are off to the hardstand where the plane is parked. Pilots check the plane for any visible problem, start the engines at the assigned time, and check them for performance. At briefed signals, we taxi along the perimeter strip to the takeoff runway, plane after plane lined up for takeoff at thirty second intervals. On the runway, hold the brakes and run up the engines before releasing the brakes to give us a kind of slingshot start. We only have 6,000 feet to get 65,000 lb or more off the ground, and every little edge helps. Crashing at the end of the runway is very serious business!

The Freckleton

Tragedy

John Threlfall

At 10:30 hours on August 23rd, 1st Lt. John Bloemendal lifted #291 clear of the runway at Warton. His crew consisted of T/Sgt. Jimmie Parr, acting as copilot, and Gordon Kinney, a Flight Test Aerial Engineer. They were accompanied by a second B-24 flown by 1st Lt. Pete Manaserro and his crew of Dick Pew and Lawrence Smith.

A few minutes into the air tests, things began to go wrong. The control tower at Warton was warned by their counterparts at Burtonwood that a violent storm was approaching from the Warrington area and that any aircraft that were airborne from Warton should be recalled immediately. The message was relayed to the two pilots, who wasted no time in plotting a course for Warton. It was then that the storm hit them.

It was the most violent storm anyone in the area had ever witnessed. People in the village of Freckleton were alarmed by its ferocity. One man stated that the rain battering against his windowpanes was so intense he could not see the houses opposite him. Jane Chestnutwood, an army nurse at the station hospital, was recovering from a bout of flu. She was off duty and resting in her quarters when the storm broke. She later stated that the intensity of the rain and lightning reminded her of the storms she had experienced in her native Indiana. To calm the children in the infant's class in the local school, their teacher was reading them a story.

Meanwhile, Lts. Bloemendal and Manaserro were fighting to control their B-24s. They were being tossed about by the hurricane-force winds in the center of the storm. They also had to contend with pitch-blackness, severe squalls, and lightning. They talked over the radio and decided to head for Scotland. It was the last Lt. Manaserro heard from Lt. Bloemendal. He could not see the other B-24, so he heaved his aircraft onto a new heading and prayed he would be able to find calmer weather conditions.

As nurse Jane Chestnutwood stood staring in the direction of Freckleton, the rain suddenly decreased to a fine drizzle and visibility became clear. It was then that she became the eyewitness of a horrific scene. A B-24 suddenly appeared from the cloudbank some five or six hundred feet above the ground. It was heading in the general direction of Warton. In the next instant it was struck by a huge bolt of lightning, which split the aircraft apart at the wing root. The two parts of the B-24 spiraled to the ground and there followed an enormous explosion. What followed next must have seemed like Armageddon to the villagers of Freckleton.

The front section of the B-24 slammed into the infant's classroom in the village school. The explosion that followed brought the whole building crashing down on the children and their teacher. To make matters worse, the aircraft had a full load of fuel on board when it took off. This fuel, now burning fiercely, covered the debris of the classroom and was also gushing down the main street of Freckleton, causing even more damage by the fires it was starting. Part of the aircraft careened across the road where it demolished a snack bar—The Sad Sack, a popular meeting place for service personnel and villagers. Of all the people who had entered The Sad Sack to shelter from the storm, there were no survivors. In all, the number of people who lost their lives through this dreadful accident was 61. This included 38 children.

The people of Freckleton have been forever grateful to the American Forces and authorities for all the help they received from them, to enable them to come to terms with this tragedy. A great bond of friendship and understanding was forged between them, and is still as strong today as it was 62 years ago when they shared each other's grief.

Author's note: For the information used in this article I am indebted to Mrs. Margaret Hall, the B.A.D. 2 Association representative in Freckleton. For the photocopied pictures, my thanks go to the staff at the Public Library in Lytham St Annes.

Oradour-sur-Glane Saturday, 10th June, 1944

Before D-Day the French Maquis had made many attacks, blowing up roads and railways and generally disrupting communications. These attacks were stepped up in the hours preceding D-Day which was notified to the waiting Maquis by the BBC, the code phrase being two lines from a poem by Verlaine.

After D-Day various reinforcements were rushed by von Rundstedt, the German commander, to plug his defenses. The II SS Panzer Division 'Das Reich' reached the Limoges area of France on 6th June.

Fourteen miles north west of Limoges lies Oradour-sur-Glane. Saturday 10 June was a busy day in the village. Apart from the village population being increased by an influx of refugees, being Saturday, many visitors had come from Limoges and surrounding villages. The village was a typical French village of gray stone houses and narrow streets.

At 2:15 p.m. a large convoy of Waffen-SS troops, wearing camouflaged green and yellow denims, drove into the village and parked in two places. The German commander was Heinz Lammerding.

Shortly afterwards the town crier announced that the entire population must assemble with identity cards in the village square. A house-to-house search was carried out to ensure everybody was there including rounding up workers in the fields. The 191 schoolchildren were told to go the church together with all the women and younger children, a group totaling 400. One small boy, Roger Godfrin, aged eight, managed to slip away to the surrounding woods.

The German Commander then announced that they were searching for Maquis arms and accordingly the men were split into six groups and taken to separate barns. Each group was guarded by several soldiers armed with sub-machine guns. Five minutes after they were there a shot was fired in the main square as a signal for the soldiers, who opened fire on the helpless prisoners. After the firing died away the soldiers picked their way between the bodies finishing off with their automatics those who still showed signs of life. The troops then covered the bodies with wood and straw and then set fire to the buildings. Only a handful of the villagers who were hidden by the bodies of their dead compatriots were able to escape.

At four p.m. soldiers entered the church where the women and children had been taken, carrying a packing case with fuses attached. These were then lit and the soldiers retired. The case exploded and produced a dense suffocating smoke. Those women that tried to escape the smoke through the chapel door to the churchyard were shot. One woman, Madame Rouffanche, managed to hide behind the altar. Here she found a stepladder and managed to climb up and squeeze through the broken middle window. A woman and child who tried to follow her were machine-gunned.

After destroying and setting fire to the other houses in the village the Germans left.

Later the Germans issued a statement to the effect that in the course of military operations Oradour-sur-Glane had been destroyed.

The village has been preserved as a memorial to the hundreds that died there. A new Oradour-sur-Glane has been rebuilt down the road. Signboards mark the location of the six buildings where the men were executed. The church still stands. The window through which Madame Rouffanche escaped is ten ft. from the ground.

The streets are silent, the tram tracks overgrown, the local garage still full of burnt out cars.

Mike's Flag

Leo K. Thorness

Submitted by Walter Mundy (467th) Condensed from a speech by Leo K. Thorness, Recipient of the Congressional Medal of Honor

You've probably seen the bumper sticker somewhere along the road. It depicts an American flag, accompanied by the words "These colors don't run." I'm always glad to see this, because it reminds me of an incident from my confinement in North Vietnam at the Hỏa Lò POW Camp, or the "Hanoi Hilton," as it became known. Then a Major in the U.S. Air Force, I had been captured and imprisoned from 1967-1973. Our treatment had frequently been brutal.

After three years, however, the beatings and torture became less frequent. During the last year, we were allowed outdoors most days for a couple of minutes to bathe. We showered by drawing water from a concrete tank with a home-made bucket. One day as we all stood by the tank, stripped of our clothes, a young Navy pilot named Mike Christian found the remnants of a handkerchief in a gutter that ran under the prison wall. Mike managed to sneak the grimy rag into our cell and began fashioning it into a flag.

Over time we all loaned him a little soap, and he spent days cleaning the material. We helped by scrounging and stealing bits and pieces of anything he could use. At night, under his mosquito net, Mike worked on the flag. He made red and blue from ground up roof tiles and tiny amounts of ink and painted the colors onto the cloth with watery rice glue. Using thread from his own blanket and a home-made bamboo needle, he sewed on stars. Early in the morning a few days later, when the guards were not alert, he whispered loudly from the back of our cell, "Hey, gang, look here." He proudly held up this tattered piece of cloth, waving it as if in a breeze. If you used your imagination, you could tell it was supposed to be an American flag. When he raised that smudgy fabric, we automatically stood straight and saluted, our chests puffing out, and more than a few eyes had tears. About once a week the guards would strip us, run us outside and go through our clothing.

During one of those shakedowns, they found Mike's flag. We all knew what would happen. That night they came for him. Night interrogations were always the worst. They opened the cell door and pulled Mike out. We could hear the beginning of torture even before they had him in the torture cell. They beat him most of the night. About daylight they pushed what was left of him back through the cell door. He was badly broken, even his voice was gone. Within two weeks, despite the danger, Mike scrounged another piece of cloth and began another flag. The Stars and Stripes, our national symbol, was worth the sacrifice for him. Now, whenever I see a flag, I think of Mike and the morning he first waved that tattered emblem of a nation.

It was then, thousands of miles from home in a lonely prison cell, that he showed us what it is to be truly free.

The Father of Aerial Bombardment

His name was Ulysses S. "Sam" Nero. He was born in Phoenixville, PA Before he finished high school, he became a rivet heater in a shipyard and went to night school to earn his high school diploma. On June 13, 1917, he enlisted in the Army and went to New Mexico to chase Pancho Villa with the 13th Cavalry. In World War I, he was in a charge of a wireless station in France with the Aviation Branch of the Signal Corps.

Back in civilian life, he took a job as a heavy equipment operator, attended night school to earn a license as a second-class engineer, and began to invent things. His best invention was a device which he called the "Nero Sight," for aiming bombs from an airplane. It allowed the Air Service to tighten a bombed area from 50-100 acres, to 10 acres. For a while, only Nero was able to use the sight accurately, but he gradually trained others to use it with a fair degree of accuracy.

At this time most of the Army's Signal Corps brass believed that bombs were more likely to hit the target when dropped from a dirigible rather than from a plane. Nero disproved this belief with a two-day test in which he dropped 37 bombs from a plane, 36 of which hit the target. In four months of trying, a dirigible crew missed every time.

In 1923, the U.S. Navy brass were adamant in their opinion that aerial bombardment could not sink a heavily-armed warship. To back up their belief, they provided two obsolete battleships, the USS New Jersey and the USS Virginia, as targets and challenged the Air Service to sink them. The test took place on September 5, 1923. Nero and his pilot, flying a Martin Curtiss NBZS-1, scored two hits on first run, but were grounded because they failed to adhere to the strict guidelines provided by the Navy.

Later in the day, when other pilots had failed to hit the targets, General Billy Mitchell asked Nero if he could do it and the answer was "Yes!" Nero and his pilot took off again and dropped a bomb down one of the New Jersey's funnels. Nothing happened for a few seconds, but then a huge explosion erupted in the bowels of the ship and three minutes later the New Jersey disappeared beneath the waves. Before landing, Nero put a bomb on the deck of the Virginia for good measure.

And so it was that Sam Nero and General Billy Mitchell proved to the embarrassed Navy brass that bombs could sink ships.

(Author unknown)

More on the Luftwaffe Sturmgruppen

After reading "Where Are Our Fighters" in the Winter 2007 *Journal*, I researched a little further and would like to add some information to the fine article from the 361st Fighter Group Newsletter.

I planned to write this by dealing solely with the Sturmgruppen and its formation in the spring of 1944. However, much had transpired in the German Air Force prior to the advent of the Sturmbock, a term formed by combining "sturm" or assault, and "bock," a male goat or ram.

A brief history should begin with the 1936-37 period and the Spanish Civil War when a number of future Luftwaffe leaders were battle-tested and German aircraft including early models of the Bf 109 were introduced—an airplane which, incidentally, then soldiered on until the Nazi regime collapsed in May of 1945!

In early September 1939, Germany attacked Poland and

unleashed WWII upon the world. The Luftwaffe reigned supreme with the Junkers Ju 87 "Stuka" dive bombers, and improved Bf 109 fighters and the Heinkel He 111 bombers. In the west the "phony war" against England and France continued until the spring of 1940 when Hitler threw his panzer divisions against France and the low countries, defeating them by mid-May of 1940. Again, the vaunted Luftwaffe ruled the skies. Eager to invade England, Hitler sent the Luftwaffe against the British Spitfires and Hurricanes in what became known as the Battle of Britain, a time period during which the Luftwaffe received its first bloody nose at the hands of the Royal Air Force.

In its inability to obtain air superiority over the English Channel, many sources believe that this situation prompted Hitler, in his impatience, to attack the Soviet Union, breaking the Hitler-Stalin Pact and creating a two-front war.

By this time, later models of the Bf 109 were in service, as well as early models of the Focke-Wulf Fw 190.

Even though the Luftwaffe had been stymied by the RAF earlier, their aircraft improved and pilots continued to hone their skills. It was over Russia that many German aces (experten) were created. It was not unusual for Luftwaffe pilots to achieve over 100 victories, some over 200 and at least five experten with over 300. Erich Hartman was at the top, ending the war with 352 victories. In late 1942 and into 1943, as the Eighth Air Force built its strength, many seasoned pilots from the Eastern Front were brought in to protect Germany's Western border.

As the turbo-supercharged B-24s and B-17s were operating at altitudes of 22,000 to 26,000 feet, both of Germany's top fighters, the Bf 109G and the Fw 190, were operating at the upper limits of their performance envelope. This war in the west was a whole new ball game for the Luftwaffe pilots. Some preferred the Eastern Front, in spite of the harsh winter conditions, to this new kind of high altitude air war against heavily armed bombers. In 1943 the attacks were usually two-plane elements firing at the bombers in running battles.

These raging battles took place beyond the range of American escort fighters, therefore, Luftwaffe losses were only to the defensive fire of the bombers.

Many tactics were tried against the four-engine American bombers *(Viermots).* One method was air-to-air bombing runs against the tight bomber formations. The head-on pass was also used until the "D" model B-24s were superseded by "H&J" models with powered nose turrets. Also, the B-17G chin turret tended to further discourage the head-on pass.

Another device tried on the Fw 190, but disliked by the pilots, were time-fused rockets of 21 cm (approximately 8-1/2" diameter) in hopes of breaking up the integrity of the tight formations.

In November 1943, Adolph Galland met with fighter commanders and informed the group that Reich Marshal Hermann Goring had ordered the establishment of the Sturmstaffel, organized to fly heavily armed fighters in close formation into the *Viermots.* The attacks, initiated from the rear, aimed to knock out the tail gunner and then use the heavy cannon to destroy the bombers at the closest possible range.

As the Luftwaffe's best hope, the Me 262 twin jet fighter, had developmental problems, the Fw 190 was being modified for this role.

Firepower increased from the Fw 190 A-5 thru the A-6, A-7 and finally the Fw 190 A-8, the ultimate Sturmbock! One of the Luftwaffe officers involved with the buildup of the Sturmstaffel and later the Sturmgruppen was Major Gunther von Kornatzki, refining the tactics and modifying the A-8 to carry the Mk 108 cannon. The firepower of this A-8 version also included two inboard MG 151/20 cannons, but it was the two outboard Mk

108s with a 33 mm shell (about 1-1/4" diameter) that made this Sturmbock an awesome weapons platform. As few as three shells striking the inboard engine and the wing root of a B-17 or B-24 would bring it down.

One Luftwaffe pilot stated that although he could shave the wing off a B-17, he believed the B-24 was structurally weaker.

After adding armor plate, bullet-proof windshield and canopy sides (blinkers), the Fw 190 A-8 could only carry aloft 55 shells for each of its two Mk 109 cannons. These airplanes were no match for the nimble P-51 escorts.

The Sturmgruppen had to rely on Bf 109 aircraft to fly top cover, as stated in the 361st Fighter Group newsletter.

It was over Oschersleben on 7 July 1944 that the Sturmgruppen hit the 492nd Bomb Group, wiping out one squadron of eleven B-24s in a little over a minute! The 2nd Air Division lost 28 B-24s that day. The worst attack was against the 445th Bomb Group on 27 September 1944 over Kassel, a mission in which the 491st was close enough for our tail gunner, Burt Blackwell, to describe the scene to the rest of us in the aircraft. We watched the 361st Mustangs fly by us to engage the Luftwaffe, but the 445th lost 25 aircraft over Eisenach.

On 26 November 1944 our own 491st was hit, losing sixteen airplanes in less than fifteen minutes. And B-17s were not immune from the carnage wrought on the 8th Air Force, as the 1st and 3rd Air Divisions were also hit hard. However, the constant losses suffered by the Sturmgruppen before the end of 1944 were unsustainable and their effectiveness diminished during the last few months of the war.

Out of one group of storm pilots, ten of thirteen would be killed, one wounded, and only two walked away from their Sturmbock.

How The Nazi Generals Justified Their Defeat

Condensed excerpts from the book The War in the Air: A Pictorial History of WWII Air Forces in Combat, *by Gene Gurney, Major USAF. Submitted by James H. Reeves (HQ)*

GOERING, CHIEF OF LUFTWAFFE:

"I knew first that the Luftwaffe was losing control of the air when the American long-range fighters were able to escort the bombers as far as Hannover. It was not long before they were getting to Berlin. We then knew we must develop the jet planes. Our plan for their early development was unsuccessful only because of your bombing attacks.

"Allied attacks greatly affected our training program, too. For instance, the attacks on oil retarded the training because our pilots couldn't get sufficient training before they were put into the air.

"I am convinced that the jet planes would have won the war for us if we had had only four or five months' more time. Our underground installations were all ready. The factory at Kahla had a capacity of 1,000 to 1,200 jet airplanes a month. Now with 5,000 to 6,000 jets, the outcome would have been quite different.

"We would have trained sufficient pilots for the jet planes despite oil shortage, because we would have had underground factories for oil, producing a sufficient quantity for the jets. The transition to jets was very easy in training. The jet-pilot output was always ahead of the jet-aircraft production.

"Germany could not have been defeated by air power alone, using England as a base, without invasion—because German industry was going underground, and our countermeasures would have kept pace with your bombing. But the point is, that if Germany were attacked in her weakened condition as now, then the air could do it alone. That is, the land invasion meant that so many workers had to be withdrawn from factory production and even from the Luftwaffe.

"We bombed cities in England instead of concentrating on aircraft and engine factories despite my original intention to attack only military targets and factories, because after the British attacked Hamburg our people were angry and I was ordered to attack indiscriminately.

"Allied precision bombing had a greater effect on the defeat of Germany than area bombing, because destroyed cities could be evacuated but destroyed industry was difficult to replace.

"Allied selection of targets was good, particularly in regard to oil. As soon as we started to repair an oil installation, you bombed it again!

"We didn't concentrate on the four-engine Focke-Wulf planes as heavy bombers after the Battle of Britain, because we were developing the He-177 and trying to develop the Me-264, which was designed to go to America and return. Because our production capacity was not so great as America's, we could not produce quickly everything we needed. Moreover, our plants were subject to constant bombing.

"If I had to design the Luftwaffe again, the first airplane I would develop would be the jet fighter—then the jet bomber. It is now a question of fuel. The jet fighter takes so much. The Me-264 awaited only the final solution of the fuel-consumption problem. According to my view the future airplane is one without fuselage (flying wing) equipped with turbine in combination with the jet and propeller.

"Before D-Day, the Allied attacks in northern France hurt us the most because we were not able to rebuild in France as quickly as at home. The attacks on marshalling yards were most effective, next came low-level attacks on troops, then attacks on bridges. The low-flying planes had a terror effect and caused great damage to our communications. Also demoralizing were the umbrella fighters, which after escorting the bombers would swoop down and hit everything, including the jet planes in the process of landing.

"The Allies owe the success of the invasion to the air forces. They prepared the invasion; they made it possible; they carried it through.

"Without the U.S. Air Force the war would still be going on elsewhere, but certainly not on German soil."

GALLAND, CHIEF OF FIGHTERS:

"In my opinion, it was the Allied bombing of our oil industries that had the greatest effect on the German war potential. Even our supplies for training new airmen was severely curtailed—we had plenty of planes from the autumn of 1944 on, and there were enough pilots up to the end of that year, but lack of petrol didn't permit the expansion of proper training to the air force as a whole.

"In the African campaign and in Sicily and Italy, Allied

successes were largely due to Allied air superiority. In my opinion, strategic bombing never forced any great change in German strategy and planning until after the opening of the invasion. Then, disorganization of German communications in the West by strategic bombing caused withdrawal to the German frontier. In the last two months of the war, the crippling of the German transport system brought about the final collapse."

KARL GERD VON RUNSTEDT, COMMANDER IN CHIEF IN THE WEST BEFORE THE GERMAN SURRENDER:

"Three factors defeated us in the West where I was in command. First, the unheard of superiority of your air force, which made all movement in daytime impossible. Second, the lack of motor fuel—oil and gas—so that the Panzers and even the remaining Luftwaffe were unable to move. Third, the systematic destruction of all railway communications so that it was impossible to bring one single railroad train across the Rhine. This made impossible the reshuffling of troops and robbed us of all mobility. Our production was also greatly interfered with by the loss of Silesia and bombardments of Saxony, as well as by the loss of oil reserves in Romania."

GEN. VON VIETINGHOFF, SUPREME COMMANDER IN SOUTHWEST (ITALY):

"On the Italian and the Western fronts, all freedom of movement for reserves and tanks was denied during daylight hours. Thus counterattacks were impossible. In isolated instances, when we were successful in assembling troops for a major surprise attack, it could only be done at night, and then the Allies were always in a position to bring their air force into action at any desired spot in a few hours and thus frustrate every German attack."

WAR DIARY OF THE 7th GERMAN ARMY HIGH COMMAND (GEN. DOLLMAN), JUNE 11, 1944:

"Since the beginning of the Allies' large-scale attack, our transport system has been under constant attack by their air forces. Because of the continuous bombing of the main roads and the constant disruption of the detours, some of which could be kept open for only a few hours, it became evident even after the first three hours that troop movements by rail could not be maintained. Infantry divisions which were being carried by rail, also had to be unloaded because the route was blocked even before they reached the army boundary line.

"Troop movements and all supply traffic by rail to the army sector must be considered as completely cut off. The fact that traffic on the front and in rear areas is under constant attack from Allied air power has led to delays and unavoidable losses in vehicles, which in turn have led to a restriction in the mobility of the numerous Panzer units due to the lack of fuel and the unreliability of the ammunition supply...

"The following information, based on the first few days' experience with the Allied deployment air power, is reported by the German Army Supreme Command:

"1. Rail transport is impossible because the trains are observed and attacked in short order: under these circumstances, the expenditure of fuel and the wear and tear on material in bringing up Panzer units is extremely high.

"2. The movement of units by motor transport is possible only at night, and even then the highways and communication centers are continually bombed. The continual control of the field of battle by Allied air forces makes daylight movement impossible and leads to the destruction from air of our preparations and attacks.

"3. The Army considers it urgently necessary that our own air force be used by day and night in order to neutralize the Allies' now unbearably overwhelming air supremacy."

Stories from London Times D-Day 50th Anniversary Issue June 5, 1994; Author Remarks; Letter from Dwight "Andy" Anderson

OK, Let's Go

When Eisenhower woke at 3:30 on the morning on June 5, the wind was shaking his trailer. After the short drive to his headquarters in Southwick House, north of Portsmouth, he listened to his weather experts, asked for opinions from his commanders, and finally, after pacing the room for what seemed several minutes to those present, quietly said: "Ok, let's go." His commanders rushed from the room to their command posts and Operation Overlord, the greatest maritime operation in history, began. From all over the south of England, landing craft carrying 132,000 men shepherded by their naval protectors gathered at the maritime equivalent of Piccadilly Circus, south east of the Isle of Wight, before swinging down "the spout" towards Normandy. The long awaited invasion was underway.

Slaughter On Omaha Beach

Robert Kershaw on the bloody fate of the first wave onto Omaha beach for whom survival became the only objective

Landing Craft Vehicle and Personnel (LCVPs) are only 36ft long and 11ft across. In each of the 48 in the first wave heading towards Omaha beach were about 30 men. There was not room for everybody to sit down and most preferred to stand – heavy backpacks made it difficult to pull themselves up from a sitting position. They had been enduring these conditions, pitching and tossing through the water, for more than three hours.

High waves washed over the ships launching for a long time. As we went in toward the beach, there was no sign of life or resistance. There was an intense quiet, so quiet it was "suspicious" through the sand dune-covered bluffs that overlooked the beach. In depth were other elements directly supported by at least three artillery batteries, numerous mortars and well-sited, heavier caliber anti-tank and field pieces.

Any hope that the preparatory bombardment had neutralized beach strong-points died 400 meters from the shore. The Germans began firing mortars and artillery fire, initially inaccurate, became increasingly effective as landing craft neared the beach. Geysers spurted up around them, blown abruptly into a fine wind-dispersed spray.

"The first ramps were dropped at 06:36," recalled Private Howard Gresser, "in water that was waist-deep."

As if this had been the signal for which the enemy waited, the ramps were instantly enveloped in crossing automatic fire that was both accurate and in great volume. It came at the boats from both ends of the beach.

Some wounded men dragged themselves ashore, lay quiet and gave themselves shots (injections of morphine), only to be caught and drowned within a few minutes by the tide.

Within a minute the second wave had piled in on top of the first. "About 75 yards from the beach the ramp was dropped and enemy automatic fire then beat a tattoo all over the boat front," reported one B Company boat.

Each man leaving the ramp was either killed or wounded. One American soldier animatedly recalled: "I didn't think that I would make it, you know, I didn't think there was any way that you could get off that beach and survive. I really thought it was my last day."

Sales was the only one to get as far as the beach. It took him two hours. Private Mack L Smith, who had been hit three times in the face, later joined him. They lay there listlessly as the fighting raged around them.

The dead washed up to where they lay and then washed back again. It was an immense physical effort for those still able to move, even to cross the beach, soaked as they were on landing.

One engineer, wading ashore with a team of 28 due to blow gaps in one of the concrete walls blocking beach exits, related: "I was coming out of the water when this guy exploded right in front of me. There just wasn't anything left of him except some of his skin, which splattered all over my arm. I remember dipping my arm in the water to wash it off."

Red-hot shards of tracer rushed up suddenly into the centre of vision, accompanied by deafening, multiple "cracks" as projectiles broke the sound barrier, displacing air at tremendous velocity as they went by. The whiplash sound is followed by the thumping report of the weapon. Bursting impacts and whining ricochets from several weapons drove men over the side of boats. "Every man acted for himself, on his own instinct," said Carroll.

Private Irwin Spandau, also on "Easy Red," saw a GI "raked with bullets across his neck. The blood came gushing out, and his head all but fell off his shoulders." It was, he says "the worst thing I had ever seen."

Sights such as these were having a debilitating effect on advancing troops who now thought less about objectives and increasingly more about survival.

Any thought of moving forward was abandoned. Only a few men were still armed and only a few of those weapons, clogged with wet sand, could fire. No leaders were there to give orders and none were given. Each man made his own decision.

At 0641 Patrol Craft 552 observing the beaches reported back to the USS Chase: "Entire first wave foundered."

Author's Comments – 448th BG

I chose excellent writings in the London Times 50th anniversary of D-Day issue June 5, 1994 about D-Day June 6, 1944. They had written about events that day that took young American lives. As I read their stories I thought "It didn't have to happen that way."

The 1 a.m. awakening of our B-24 crew was to be one of the roughly 2200 bombers targeted to destroy German firepower against American troops landing on the beach. My worry was a collision with another bomber in the dark and crowded sky. We never found our intended group. It didn't matter—we were all going to the same place.

Each of the 2200 bombers had a crew of ten, or 22,000 men. How many bombers did we lose that day? Two to collisions, one to enemy action, one to explosion, and one who crashed after takeoff in England. A portion of these would have parachuted, so I surmised that no more than half or 25 were killed. Contrast that down there where the Germans were throwing lots of lead at the invading force. There were 15,000 casualties by June 8, the vast majority on Omaha Beach. Why? 1. German guns, German troops, mostly untouched; and 2., troops dropped off in deeper water (up to 6 feet) by the landing craft and other troop carrier crews. Soldiers with rifles, and other gear drowned. The beach was loaded with land mines.

Because we flew over the ships and landing craft on our way to drop bombs, we were warned not to drop early. We didn't. We dropped late, and overshot big German guns on the hill and machine guns in the sand dunes' valleys. Our bombs overshot the bombing target area and landed in cow pastures.

The answer to me was bomb one half-hour – or more before troops would hit the beach and not to fly north to south but east to west over German defenses, the big hill above the beach and the sand dune valleys where German machine guns could crossfire into our disembarking force. Out of 22,000 bombers, a number would drop a few seconds early or others a few seconds late and severely damage and kill on a mile that the Germans could no longer use as effectively.

Even with these suggestions Omaha Beach would remain

difficult. We would not have killed all the defenders, but instead of thousands of casualties it could have been kept in the hundreds.

A tragedy a few days before D-Day were two landing barges on a training mission some thirty or so miles north of Omaha Beach. They were attacked by two German gunboats who were able to sink the two barges with the result – 600 American troops drowned. The Royal or American navy was not present, nor was air power over the site for protection.

Yes, they did get up the cliff (thanks to Rangers) and to the hedge rows. They were another obstacle that the army was not prepared to counter. American ingenuity made changes to tanks to accomplish the tasks. That's another story about war on the ground, which I know little about. My war was in the air. For my write-up on the only time I flew two missions the same day, June 6, 1944, see "My 33 Missions" in Bombs Away! Volume I. The target for the second mission was to destroy a bridge which the German infantry would use to meet the Omaha Beach invasion.

A few words about our combat training. I was extremely fortunate by sheer chance to have assigned to my crew of ten these key positions. 1. Engineer – Isadore Buechner, born, lived, died in Cross Plains, Wisconsin. See "Issy was a Hero" which I wrote and sent to the Madison, Wisconsin newspaper. 2. Bombardier – Philip Goplen, Minnesota native, only other member of our crew still alive. He was armament officer which meant that when bottom bombs piled up it was his duty to kick these out so that the bombs above would not pile up. You're 20,000 feet in the air, the enemy is shooting at you, the narrow catwalk could be slippery with a hydraulic leak, it's twenty below zero and you need to carry an oxygen bottle. There is no room for you to wear a chest pack parachute. You can see the ground four miles below you as you rectify the situation. After some missions Phil would tell how a particular bombardier would hit the target every time.

It's difficult to always know exactly where you are over France or Germany. Our navigator, Frank Erbacher from Ohio, would be asked by the lead navigator upon our return from a mission where we had been on a Cook's Tour. "Frank, where the hell were we today?" He knew.   We were asked if we wanted to be a lead crew – not because of me, but Frank. I put it to the crew. Lead crews did not fly every mission and our guys, to a man, said "Let's get it over with as soon as possible." My sentiments exactly (See another crew decision on a mission to Berlin, my most memorable combat mission).

I had a very pleasant assistant engineer, Vince Torfin, Minnesota. Snyder twins from Baltimore. Their parents said to the army to keep them together. The tail gunner was a bit incorrigible, the waist gunner, fine. Tex, ball turret gunner, TX. Worst job on the crew but the turret did not need to be extended unless fighters were in the area. We were lucky. We saw a few German fighters but lots of flak, and more as German ground troops kept moving east with their guns…. Our radio operator was a fine young fellow from Virginia. He was not meant for war. He would cover himself with flak jackets. Shortly before finishing our tour, he had to be relieved of his duties. War was too much for him I liked this young man and we went on our leave together to Dollar, Scotland.

I must add this – I'd rather do two of my 33 mission tours than one of the early 25 mission tours. They had it really tough—lots of German fighters, and it was more time before we deployed the great P51 (but in the latter part of 1940 the Germans came up with a fighter jet).

We had visited the cemetery at Omaha Beach some twenty years ago before there was a museum. We returned and I left a book with the office and started to walk down the museum. The manager caught up with me and we had a pleasant conversation. I later learned that he was assigned to the U.S. Embassy in Paris and they had deployed him to this museum. Here is a letter I received from him.

Hello Mr. Welsh —

I would just like to take the opportunity to wish you and your family all the best for the season and Happy New Years. I just recently finished reading your book which you were so kind to send me. From it I learned a lot of new stories of soldiers buried in our cemeteries. I shared those with the respective cemeteries. Our job here at the ABMC is to keep the grass green, the headstones white and tell the stories of the soldiers buried here. The motto of the ABMC is a quote from Gen. Pershing "Time will not dim the glory of their deeds." From reading your book I almost feel as if I know you and your love of life can only come I think from people such as ourselves who have experienced that insidious thing called "war." We had a saying in Vietnam, "Life has a special flavor the protected shall never know." I wish you many more years of all the best.

Military Experiences
of Bob Mallas

I was drafted into the army as I reached 18, weighed only 104 lbs., but was 5"10" tall. I was knowledgeable of the war and its challenges to our nation and way of life. My father was from an important Greek family and fled to the U.S. when his father, a key Greek government official, was killed when the government was overturned. He loved this country and wanted me to serve. I had 17 weeks of basic training in the infantry, was shipped from Boston in a huge convoy of ships. After 20 days of sub alerts we docked in Cherbourg, loaded onto trucks for a 10-day trip to the 99th Division on the front lines. I had contracted pneumonia, and my foxhole buddy reported my illness and the company commander ordered me back to regiment for medical attention. This was 2 a.m., December 15, 1944. Four hours later the 99th and our company was attacked by a major German force. It killed the buddy who was instrumental in saving my life. I was transferred to a medical center some 40 miles behind the front line, a very busy M.D. pronounced me as a goner, but the nurse got permission to give me some new drugs. They were effective, but German troops in the area required the evacuation of the hospital. As all the trucks had left, walking was the only alternative. With a good supply of pills, I started down the road to where the Americans were supposed to be, and on 22 December, I hooked up with the 69th Division, and was sent to the hospital immediately. So, from December 19 until January 3 about all I know is that I ended up about 60 miles from where I started, and with the 69th Division, where I spent the rest of the war. But it was a Christmas season not remembered!

The 69th moved into a defensive position on the Siegfried Line, replacing another division badly mauled during the Bulge. On our left was the remains of another division that had lost two thirds of its men during the Bulge. The Lt. platoon leader came back from company headquarters with a manual on radios, handed it to me, announcing I would be the new radio man. I didn't find this a welcome decision in that all our radiomen had been killed the last three days... If not on patrol, I was radioman for an outpost several hundred feet in front of our lines set up to detect any attack. Although the Germans were in retreat, they were contesting every inch. As we neared the Rhine, the tension grew since we had heard all the bridges were destroyed and the Germans were prepared to contest any crossing.

On March 8 we reached the west side of the Rhine. On the 9th, word came that a group of engineers had seized a bridge at Remagen, about nine miles to the north, and we had to cross the river and strike north to clear out their front. We crossed in little rubber boats across the wide Rhine, no shooting, the Germans had retreated. We were off to assist our troops at Remagen.

Unfortunately, we had no transportation since tanks and trucks could not get over on temporary bridges for at least another 48-72 hours and we had to immediately attack north to force the

Germans away from the bridge. Because about two-thirds of our company were in the early stages of recovering from badly frozen feet, fresh troops were more directly involved in the attack to save the bridgehead. Suddenly the forces to our front collapsed and we had to move up as fast as we could, 76 miles on foot, in three days with full 65 pounds of equipment. One could not drop out since if you did the large number of German soldiers in the forests around us would have killed anyone alone.

Marching distances with full gear presented another problem. With frozen feet one cannot get shoes on right away, so we walked in our overshoes. With the swelling receding, shoes can be worn by cutting open the sides. However, foot bone structure begins to break down, pain increases, until the foot goes numb. Continuing, it feels like you are stepping on your ankles, and then your knees. Stopping, the pain is intense as circulation returns. We were not a good fighting force at the end of those 76 miles, but again luck was on our side. A group of heavy tanks had crossed the Rhine and joined us. We rode them to a key railroad junction, and thousands of displaced persons (slave laborers) lined the road greeting us. The road into town was narrow, I was on the second tank. The first tank was about 30 feet ahead, about ready to make a tight turn when suddenly from a balcony right above the tank a woman drops a chamber pot and its contents down on the tank, spilling on the sergeant in charge. Before we could react she disappeared into the building. The tank stopped, the sergeant barked out an order, the tank backed up about 20 feet and as it went forward it cut into the side of the building, tearing out the first story, causing the second story to collapse. I guess you might say she made her statement, and the sergeant his.

Two mornings later we rode tanks down a road with thick forest on each side. The tank had lost its 50-caliber machine gunner the day before, and the tank commander asked if anyone could fire that gun. Two knew how, myself and a 46 year old guy whose feet were in very bad condition. I was chosen. Suddenly there was heavy fire. In combat, contrary to the movies, the infantry dismounts and clears out the enemy since the tank is much more valuable. I left the tank and went with the infantry, and the 46 year old took over the gun. He had false teeth. A sniper shot him and the bullet hit him in the lower teeth, curved around, cut his upper lip badly, and came out. The force almost broke his neck. I was stunned to see him running down the center of the road spitting blood and false teeth, firing into the trees to try to find that sniper, and cursing words I had never heard.

Next day we captured a concentration camp which was set up in central Germany for displaced persons who could no longer work, or were sentenced to be killed... A few days later a small group of Germans gave themselves up and told us that our President was dead. We were so far ahead of our supply lines that news (and sometimes rations) did not get to us for days. My radio was effective for only a few miles. Our attitude was "typical Nazi crap." We were stunned when a truck with ammo and food came in the next day and confirmed their story. Major groups of Germans began to surrender. Three elite Hungarian regiments (about 9,000 men) immediately to our front refused to fight U.S. troops. While we had hit and run type action, each day we knew it was just a matter of time until the European war was over.

The next night Sergeant M. handed me a thick letter. He was an outstanding soldier in every respect, and one of the few in our company that, like myself, started at the Siegfried and still survived. He said "I know this sounds silly, but for some time I have known I would not survive the war. Here is my will and a letter to my folks. You will survive! Please get it to them and go see them when you get back to the states." He asked for my promise, and that I gave.

Three nights later we were in a tough house-to-house fight in Colditz—the last remaining link between the Germans in Berlin and those in the south. It also was the location of an old castle that held several hundred top allied prisoners of war, and we were told they were to be killed. To get to the castle we had to cross over a deep stream, with the bridge still intact. In the dark the twisting streets leading to the bridge were death traps. Suddenly, the Germans pulled out and rushed across the bridge. We felt the way was open. We lined up scouts in front, the lieutenant and I next on the left, and Sergeant M on the right. The street took a sharp turn to the right and Sergeant M realized that when the Lt. and I turned the corner we would be most exposed. He motioned for us to change spots.

As we were doing so, a shot from a basement window rang out. I saw Sergeant M. Freeze, and the lieutenant and I fired several shots into the sniper. As I turned around, the sergeant fell into my arms. The shot hit him under the chin and came out the temple. He was dead. I followed his wishes to the letter, but how did he know he would die?

We stopped as we got to the bridge. Too dark and risky. Was the bridge mined? All during the night the guards at the center of the bridge changed every four hours. As soon as they got to the center we would pick them off and they would fall into the water—all except the one who lay on the bridge. Obviously, the Germans were confused and the command structure was breaking down as the regular German units were pulling out.

The next morning, we could see the bridge was not mined, and all was quiet. As we went up on the bridge a mother was loading her dead 15 year old son into a little cart. He was the guard that did not fall into the water. The G.I.s helped her.

We got to the castle and liberated the still-alive prisoners of war. At the last minute the SS pulled out and left no instructions for them to be killed, and the prison commander was not about do so now that the end was in sight.

A jeep roared up and the driver said, "Anyone here know how to work the 300 (radio)?" Everyone pointed at me and he said "Get in." He was a lieutenant and wanted to know if I spoke any Russian. I said no, but could speak some French. In a little square were a group of G.I.s of several ranks. All like myself had not bathed or shaved or changed clothes in over four months. Three jeeps, an armored personnel carrier, several types of trucks and tanks began to come in. It turned out there were to be three groups whose mission was to try to rush through the weakly held German lines, about 15-20 miles, to the Elbe River to meet the Russians, who were advancing from the east. Our group rushed headlong toward the Elbe, brushing aside minor resistance. Soon I started picking up a strange language on the radio and our experts identified it as Russian. As morning came, we confirmed they were across the Elbe at Torgau. By the middle of the afternoon we made actual contact. Fortunately, they were even dirtier than we were. It was April 25th—my sister's 23rd birthday. Soon the press was with us taking pictures. As I write this I am looking at the framed front page of the New York Times dated April 28, 1945. Two G.I.s with hands outstretched are greeting four Russian soldiers. The reproductions are poor. I am wearing a helmet that covers part of my face and it is hard for me to see me in the photograph. Much to my surprise a letter from my mother told me my picture had been in Life magazine, the Toledo Blade, and the Cleveland Plain Dealer (the same picture). She recognized me! When I saw the picture I realized that only a mother would ever be able to do that! Only one of the ways mothers are truly remarkable!!!

The Russians shared food, drink, music, dancing and, to the horror of the G.I.s, —kisses. As noted, we were filthy, but they were even worse. They all seemed to have lots of lice and if they were not drinking, they were scratching. Soon, we all were—drinking and scratching.

Since there were no others from my company at this Elbe River meeting with the Russians, it was time to return, and a driver was dispatched to pick me up. He said "You've got a sweet deal. It's guarding Germany's largest ammunition/poison gas dump." So for the first time in months I had a bed (a straw filled mattress cover on the floor), a bath, and clean clothing. All except the officers were quartered in one huge stone room at the center of the ammo dump.

On May 8 all of us—approximately 100 remaining out of full company strength of 186 -except those on guard duty were in that large room, and a BBC news flash came on announcing the ceasefire signing. I looked around the room. In one card game a hand ready to play a card was suspended. No sounds, except the noise of celebration in London, Paris, and New York. Then the arm descended and the card was played. But there was no talking, as each was deep in thoughts. But off to my right I heard a quiet sobbing. Those of us who heard it pretended not to notice. Sitting on his mattress with back to the wall was Sergeant "N," without question the most fearless fighter in the group. He volunteered for every dangerous mission, and had been decorated four times. If he had a fault it was that he never took a prisoner. He loved to kill. The time he could kill and be accepted was gone. With his depression he was sent back for treatment. I hope they could help him, but I often wondered if he ended up as a hit man for organized crime, or a serial killer.

Bear in mind that only one in seventeen in service in WWII had any contact with combat, and only one if fifty were actually part of any group that lost men in combat. This does not mean that their support was any less vital or their contribution less important, but it does mean their viewpoint is different. Often combat veterans do not want to discuss what happened to them.

During the 1950s I did much research on mental illness and mental health programming. The study went on for over two years, and one of the great minds involved had spent time and effort studying battle fatigue cases. He noted that much time and money had been spent on those that combat "broke" mentally, but almost nothing on those who mentally survived. He said that the important thing is what happens mentally if you survive past the statistical point where you should be dead, and realize it. As days go by surviving you make a mental adjustment, and achieve what he called "psychiatric death." The life you were in you have accepted as ended, and you are now in a new life with death no longer a concern.

I feel that the room was so quiet on the announcement of the war's end was that many had achieved fully, or in part, such a mental position. They had tried to end that part by making a mental adjustment.

Three Incidents
Relative to Combat
Soldiers
Bob Mallas, Continued

Our company was to take a key railroad location. We moved into position, found out the Germans had artillery, and we none. They must have had too few troops for an attack on us, and because we were outgunned it was a standoff. Our artillery didn't get in place until 5 p.m., which caused the German tanks to leave. We were ordered to fire as rapidly as possible as we charged across the farmland into the town, to force any German soldiers to take cover and not fire on us.

It turned out they had left with the tanks. We had to search all the houses for hiding enemy soldiers. Near the edge of town was a large, nice looking home. It was not locked and a group of six of us, including the Lieutenant, surrounded it. Instructions were to search all three floors... we knew what to look for... especially booby traps. The search showed no one in any of the three floors, so we relaxed a bit. Suddenly the Lt. pointed to the corner of the living room where we had gathered. Not easily seen was a trapdoor.

The Lt. motioned us into position and guardedly opened the trap door and called down in German "hands overhead." Immediately we could hear movement and all of our weapons were at the ready. One old-time pro suggested we throw a few grenades down into the cellar, and move on. The Lt. said no, let's give them a chance to surrender. Our Sgt., who spoke German, told them to surrender. We could hear movement on the stairs and the first person to come out was a very little girl clutching a doll, followed by a small boy, two children in their early teens, mother, father, and one much older person. I told the Lt. "Just think, 2 grenades would have killed them all!" He replied, "Right, but keep in mind if they tossed two grenades up here we would all have been killed or wounded."

Another happening was at the Siegfried line and word came down that the Germans were preparing to attack. High command wanted the answers to a number of questions, and the only way we could get those was a night patrol into the German lines to capture soldiers. The Lt. was to be the patrol leader, I the radio man, and six others for specific skills, such as mines, language, use of weaponry. "Rich" was chosen because he was the best sharpshooter in the company, and had unlimited skills needed for patrols. He had lied about his age to get in the army, and was only 16 years old. Born in the interior of Alaska of a very poor family almost all the food they ate came from hunting, shooting if they had ammunition money, but mostly from trapping. The family consisted of his parents and a grandmother. None had gone to school, or could read and write. Rich had gone to school a year before the army when they moved to Montana. His dad got a defense job. A retired teacher in the area heard of Rich's needs and taught him to read and write a bit. Rich understood his limitations, was friendly with a great smile, and always listened and tried to be helpful. He was well liked and ALL understood that when it came to arms, hunting and the out-of-doors, he was the expert in our group. The Lt. asked him for suggestions for our patrol mission. Contrary to a normal setup, Rich suggested one scout in front, another in back, and the Lt. and me in the center with a rifleman. Rich would stay about 6 feet to the rear of the front scout. There were patches of fog and snow falling now and then, with just enough light to see outlines some 20 feet ahead. We had just gotten through the first belt of mines when suddenly Rich stopped and signaled for us to get prone quietly. What seemed like a long time, but probably only a few minutes, he lifted his hand and signaled be VERY QUIET. Another few minutes went by and we could hear someone walking on the snow, and talking quietly.

Quietly Rich got up on one knee and fired three times as rapidly as possible. Each shot killed each German scout, and the officer in charge. A German fired back, and Rich fired once more and that German was dead. The last two Germans surrendered... Our patrol was a success since they quickly gave us the German plans.

We asked Rich later how he knew they were there and he said "I heard them." None of the rest of us did. We had questions as to how could he know how many, the formation they were in and how could he see to fire so quickly. It all boiled down to all those years of outsmarting game so they could eat. He was awarded the Silver Star for that mission. I understand that he stayed in the army, went to night school, and became a trainer for our special forces, an intelligent use of his skills.

In the third story, we got to a small German town and set up a guard on all sides, sort of like a wagon train preparing to fight Indians. The tank group had its own cook and in the town square, he sat up his kitchen. Small groups of us would come in and eat, while other groups were on guard. The German civilians were very watchful and since we treated them well they grew more relaxed with us. Some of them came out and watched us eat. We noted that a group of children, most under the ages of 10-12, had set up a line near the place we went to dispose of any food left in our mess kits. We understood they were short of food and we were trying to save a bit for them. The children were also interested in the coffee and were standing with a container in each hand... one for the coffee and the other to get any food scraps.

Just before we crossed the Rhine we had gotten a small number of replacements just in from the states. One in particular (his name was Jim) was boastful, never listened, and made few, if any friends. I think we all knew with his attitude he would not last through much combat.

Four of us were walking toward the point where the German children were waiting and three (including Jim) were just ahead of us. Jim was in the lead and when he got to the first child... a five or six year old boy... he poured his hot coffee over the boys' hands saying something like 'take this, you God damn Nazi!" Instantaneously... and I mean faster than any quick draw you will see in a Western movie... the fellow at the head of our group drew his 45 and had it at Jim's temple. None of us moved. We knew that old combat pro could shoot without hesitation.

About thirty seconds went by and with gun in hand he ordered Jim to his knees, threw him a rag, and told him to wipe off the boys' hands. Jim did just as he was told. Fortunately, the coffee was not hot enough to burn the boy. The German children and adults were very carefully watching. My Lt. took Jim to the side and gave him a strict lecture. Jim felt he knew better. As predicted, he was killed a short time later... One can conclude from these three stories that those in combat were very much like men we see each day. They brought to combat the standards and knowledge mostly taught prior to the war.

The Holland Trip...
The Reaction of One
of Our Allies

In my last military duty in Europe through circumstances I was able to meet and be of value to our General. He repaid me by continuing to add to my stripes as I completed special assignments. One of these was the delivery of secret documents (I did not see them) to a key British General in Holland and, as a personal favor, visiting a nearby military cemetery and take pictures of a grave for the mother of a soldier buried there.

Once again I had a jeep with jeep-trailer to carry gasoline and all supplies, including food for the trip. The driver and I were fully armed since any trip was dangerous in those days. We over-nighted at a base on the edge of our U.S. sector and got everything done the next day.

The cemetery had all the graves indexed and we found the proper grave for photos easily. I was able to find three graves of those I had served with during "The Battle of the Bulge." A sad experience. On the way out to the cemetery along both sides of the road were people carrying flowers. Not just a few, but many—men, women, and children. At the cemetery we saw a vast number of graves with flowers. Cemetery staff told us this was a daily ritual and had been going on even before the war had ended. These people were truly grateful.

The most important display of gratitude happened after we left the cemetery. I could smell something burning. One of the back tires had given way and was slipping on the rim, and smoking. We stopped the jeep and almost immediately one front tire blew out, and the other back tire went flat. We had hit something in the road. There we were in the middle of Holland, in the British Sector, and three flat tires but only one spare.

On the road's opposite side was a little business operation with two men out front looking at us. One young man, not more than 18-19—but tall in size, started across the road toward us. Both the driver and I were armed but the young man was smiling and looked friendly. He saw the problem. I tried to speak to him in English, and then French, but he did not understand either. He put his hand to his ear and motioned to the business place and for us to stay where we were. He went back and phoned, and came back all smiles.

It turned out the U.S. had an MP (military police) station about 40 miles away. It was in the British Sector to help police monitor stolen goods movement. Two weeks before they had seized a stolen jeep and impounded it. When they got the call they understood our need. They took the tires off the jeep for our use... Once they ascertained via our papers we were okay, they gave us the tires and took off. We started to put the tires on but the young man pointed to our uniforms, shook his head, and picked up the tools and started the job. I said to the driver, "Let him do it... he has earned a good fee already."

In record time the tires were replaced. I took out some money and several packages of cigarettes worth around $150 on the black market. When I offered them his face fell and I thought for a moment it was not enough and offered more. He shook his head, stood up very straight, and saluted us! Both of us were stunned. When I recovered I extended my hand and shook his hand and said thank you. I motioned for him to come to the trailer. In it we had some candy bars and other snack goodies. When I handed him a candy bar he looked at it and as I peeled the wrapper off he did so also, but saved the wrapper. I noted he ate two small bites and wrapped the balance up. In looking at him and his reaction to the food I noted that, though tall, he was VERY thin. I got an idea. I told the driver to pick up all the extra food and cigarettes from the trailer, and with our arms full we walked across the road to the door of the business. Inside was an older lady and man, a young girl, and two children 14-16 years of age.

From a quick glance I could see all were very thin. We put the food and over four cartons of cigarettes on a table. (Cigarettes could buy anything, while money usually would not.) We gave a candy bar to each and the driver and I pulled out our partially eaten bar, showing that it was safe to eat. Watching that half-starved family enjoy that candy... especially the younger children... is a life-long memory. What was especially meaningful was the young man was doing all that work out of affection for what our troops had done to liberate his country. Later I learned each soldier buried at that cemetery had been adopted by a Dutch family who kept flowers on their grave summers. I noted their name and address before we left. My driver, who talked very little, told me that such an experience of appreciation and gratitude made fighting the war worthwhile...

The General was impressed when I related the happening to him. He called in his secretary and told her to phone a Colonel and

I heard him relate the incident, and how we wanted to help that family. I heard the General say "I think 20 cartons will give them enough buying power to last a couple of years... and have that M.P group deliver them in person." Later I asked the secretary who the Colonel was, and she said he headed all the PX (post exchange) operations in the U.S. Sector!

From Bomber

Legends

Reading *Bomber Legends* rekindles memories of escorting B-17s and B-24s into the territorial belly occupied by Germany.

My stateside training for combat was some 50 hours in the razorback P-47, firing nary a shot. We did get considerable low-level navigation flights which was invigorating to skim at tree top level or below, but likely not amusing to the local residents who endured our devilish tactics.

Debarking at Tripoli, quickly found myself near the village of San Severo, westerly of Foggia at the spur of Italy. Displaying my best 2nd Lt salute to the squadron commander, Major Lee Wiseman, I was informed to take a short flight in the P-38. I had never seen a P-38 or been in the cockpit of a twin engine aircraft, so I asked for the Pilot's Operating Manual. He stated there was no manual available and move as I was scheduled for a mission.

Checked out a parachute, oxygen mask and canvas helmet and was jeeped to a P-38 where the crew chief instructed me on the procedure for getting to the cockpit by opening a retractable scissor-like ladder at the trailing end of the gondola fuselage. Settling into the cockpit, the crew chief reached over and started the engines. I felt at home in the cockpit. At the end of the dirt runway, which was the width of a residential street and some 2000 feet long at best, pushed the throttles forward and was impressed by the purr of 1400 horsepower on each side. With no external load, the counter-rotating props thrust me into the air in short order. This was love at first flight.

My first mission was a short strafing run in northern Italy, staying on the deck until reaching the target. The next day was an exposure to our primary mission; escorting long-range bombers, this time to Ploesti. Awoke that morning to the distant sound of bombers herding into formations and heading to the target. After a hefty breakfast – there were no snacks for the next five hours or more – the skies were silent as we were briefed on our role in protecting the bombers; namely, do not get sucked into a battle that would expose the bombers to assault. Briefly, we were to position between the bombers and any enemy aircraft, entering into battle only if the bombers were threatened. The more agile P-51s were responsible for engaging the enemy fighters.

Our flight became airborne some two hours after the bombers set course for the target area. We would rendezvous with the bomber formations about 150-200 miles from the target. Over the bomber formation, reduced RPM and increased the manifold pressure to conserve fuel. My more experienced tent mate instructed me on this procedure, which was passed over from Charles Lindbergh who was flying the P-38 in the Pacific area. We stayed two to three thousand feet above the bomber string in lazy S turns to stay abreast of the bombers and have better sight for enemy fighters.

The temperature inside the cockpit was the same as the outside temperature – damn cold – 50 to 60 degrees below zero.

I had traded my leather jacket for British fur-lined boots, but my feet were numb. Looking down on the graceful B-17s I began to absorb the plight of the crews jammed in a tube of thin aluminum at subzero temperature and sitting on several tons of explosives. Aggravating were the bursts of antiaircraft fire over the target – Ploesti – incessant blasts of fire leaving a thick cloud of black smoke. I agonized for the crews that flew into that pulsating mass of firepower with its attendant shrapnel. It did not seem plausible that any aircraft could survive such compact antiaircraft defense. No words or monuments can adequately portray the skill and courage of those bomber crews.

Nearing the flak area, we broke off coverage. Fighter pilots may not be the most intelligent lot, but neither the allied or German fighters penetrated the flak zone. While skirting the target area I noted a conspicuously large burst of flak which I reported in my intelligence debriefing. Only on a later mission did I realize those bursts were bombers receiving a direct hit in the bomb bay. We would pick the bombers up as they exited, often scattered vertically and horizontally. The German fighters preyed on stragglers or crippled aircraft. It was at this stage that we were more likely to engage the enemy.

Believe it was on my sixth escort mission to Ploesti that I was separated from my flight short of the target area, so maneuvered to the north to pick up any stragglers. Obviously too close to the flak zone, my plane took a hit in the right engine, which I feathered while pushing the throttle forward on the left engine to retain airspeed. The power in the left engine diminished, inadequate to maintain altitude, thus began a slow descent toward home, some 500 plus miles distance. My objective was to reach Yugoslavia, bail out and have the local tribes return me home through a U.S. friendly network.

Heading away from Ploesti, the visibility was unlimited and

no other aircraft were in sight; it was like someone flipped a switch and the war was over. It was an eerie sensation being in a war zone of tranquility – and a bit lonely. I grasped the placid beauty of the quilt of farmlands and villages basking in an admixture of midsummer greens and scattered patterns of gray and brown. At about 15,000 feet, I could maintain altitude at a comfortable speed above stalling. However, I felt like a piñata hanging on a heavenly string awaiting someone to swat me.

In that moment of mixed emotions – serene anxiety – observed a crippled B-17 several miles to my left and eased toward it cautiously so as not to be mistaken for a German at the controls. In North Africa there were reports of downed U.S. planes being repaired, and German pilots mischievously attacking allied planes. Hanging off the right wing of the B-17, the waist gunner waved and I signaled in return, comforted by the protection of their gunners and relaxed knowing some 16 or so other eyes were scanning the skies, allowing me to check my instruments and calculate my fuel and position for the flight home... I wondered how this would look on my fighter pilot resume: "Crippled B-17 escorts fighter to safety." At that juncture, I didn't care.

Am unaware how long I ambled along under the protective wing of that B-17 – seemed like hours. As we approached the mountains of Yugoslavia, I drifted down and away, picking up speed. Shortly, the gleaming Adriatic reflected the sun streams and some small boats were hugging the crusty shore, a scene that made me complacent. That was short lived as some tracers altered my composure, dictating some modest evasive action. I was directly over Spit where the Germans harbored one of the elite antiaircraft units. I assume most of the soldiers had called it quits for the day as I was an easy target. From there it was clear sailing.

I wonder if that B-17 crew made it back okay and are readers of *Bomber Legends.* I'd like to thank them for their hospitality and security of the escort.

My B-24 Experience

Hazel Hohn, Woman's Airforce Service Pilot

From *Bomber Legends*.

I think maybe the only thing interesting about my flying B-24 Liberators during World War II is that I was a female pilot. I don't think there too many of them, so I will write about it. After graduating from Avenger Field, Sweetwater, Texas in May, 1944, as a WASP (Women's Airforce Service Pilot). I was assigned to the Air Transport Command in Romulus, Michigan, hoping to become a fighter (pursuit) pilot. First we checked out in UC78s and Noorduyn Norsemans and after one flight around the field in the nose of a 24, I went directly to the copilot seat on ferry trips. We picked up the 24s from the factory at Willow Run. I understand they were putting out a 24 every hour and there were usually no test or other flights before we got them. Hence, we were actually production test pilots, though I never thought of us as such until long after the war. I remember that often the autopilot would not work.

My first trip was the pilot's 2nd trip, and he was so nervous he actually shook. Here he gets a totally inexperienced WASP as copilot. If it weren't for the flight engineer, I don't think we would have gotten to our destination. Actually, we started to land at the wrong base, and the engineer called our attention to it. From there, we picked up other 24s to deliver to other bases, and by the time we finished we knew what we were doing.

I had a different left seat pilot each time, so had to adjust to their expectations of me. But usually as soon as we got to altitude and synchronized our engines, he and the engineer would go back somewhere and play cards. I would slide over to the left seat and fly the plane to the destination. This made me feel pretty proud—all that horsepower, when I had been flying Cubs a short time before. It was also amusing to see men's faces when we would land at a base and I'd come out of that big plane.

One thing that made my flying 24s unique is that when they were shipped to Europe to bomb Germany, underneath were my future husband and in-laws, who were German nationals during the war. The men all fought on the Eastern front, as far as I know, and one was captured and sent to Siberia. My husband was in the Hitler Youth, and he said he would lie in bed wondering "Why are they doing this to me? I'm just an innocent kid." Little did he know the plane might have been delivered by his future wife. I heard about this from time to time. My sister-in-law's father, a Luftwaffe fighter pilot, was shot down and killed by an American fighter. Such is war. It seemed strange at first to visit the former "enemy" but that didn't last long. However, visiting my sister in law on the North Sea (Husum) which was always foggy, I would think of those bombers and the fog on those raids which I had heard so much about during the war.

Dinghy, Dinghy, Let's Ditch Properly, and Live

Written by the author. After finishing his mission tour, he became a group air-sea rescue officer. He wrote this for present and future crews.

CP ( )   B ( )   RO ( )   RWG ( )   TG ( )
N ( )   E ( )   LWG ( )   BTG ( )

First — if you're over water and ditching seems probable, get rid of your excess weight. If danger is imminent, throw out all loose equipment. You don't want to get clipped by a loose piece of junk lying around at what starts out at 100 m.p.h. when you stop. Take off your parachute. Don't inflate your Mae West. Wear a steel helmet.

Radio operator — be sure your trailing antenna is out — if not, the ground stations won't be able to get a decent fix. Also, turn your IFF to emergency.

Pilots — call Mayday, mayday, Mayday, this is Egress (be sure to use squadron call sign — there may be ten D for Dogs ditching) D Dog. Come, in; Colgate, over. When they come in, give them the desired poop — course, alt, A/S, position, R/D, and a long count. In a very short time they may give you a new heading, as much as 30 degrees different than the present one you are flying. Use it — they will either be steering you over rescue boats or to nearer land. (Remember, they always give you mag headings). If you aren't in serious trouble, get off the air and let some Joe who's really in trouble sing his song. However, if you are in serious trouble, make frequent calls.

Second — you're going to hit the water now. Remember, pilot, that the less speed you have the less you're going to bang your men up. With a light airplane and 40 degrees of flaps there's no reason why it can't be brought down at 100 m.p.h. or less (no, I've never done it). The speed at which you hit the water is proportional to the breakage of the plane — and these 24s do break up — there are some places you don't want to be, so assume the proper positions.

In the cockpit the pilot and copilot should have their Sutton harnesses on, with their seat locked in the forward position. If you have armor plate, stand a man on each side, with your back covered by support from the base of your spine to the top of your head. In case there is no head support, clasping your hands behind your head will take a force up to 26 x gravity force. You can sit between the legs of those against the armor plate, but do not have anyone on the floor — that turret probably will come down. If there is no armor plate, the back of the pilot's seats will have to be used. The radio operator can use the strap on his seat to protect his head.

In the waist, the ditching belts are the best bet. If they are not installed, use a six-man support — two facing forward with legs braced against the nine steps of the ball turret, and two braced against each side, with arms of all six locked. This position has been tried and proven safe.

After you hit the water, you know what to do. Nevertheless, an appalling number of men come out of the crash okay only to get washed away in the sea, and with a rubber dinghy it's next to impossible to rescue you. Remember to bring along the needed emergency equipment, and also to pull the life raft release handles. If you're unable to get inside the plane, there are emergency handles on top of the fuselage.

Now — if you see someone else about to ditch or ditching, lend him a hand. If you have enough gas, circle him at altitude — 5000 feet if you are 25 miles or less from the English coast, and 8000 feet if out further. Then send in his position. You can use your VHF and MFDF.

In summary — if ditching, rid the plane of all objects possible; be sure to assume the correct ditching position, well braced; lastly, it's the pilot's baby — remember that slow touchdown speeds will have a big part in saving your crew.

From "Before I say Adieu"

Earl E. Wassom, 466th, Past President

The B-24 was a great airplane, but we lost many of them. A typical bomber lasted only 147 days. The Eighth Air Force logged 6,537 heavy bombers lost and 3,337 fighter aircraft destroyed. The B-24 brought many, but not all of us, home.

When the conflict ended in 1945, almost 7,000 of our Second Air Division had made the ultimate sacrifice. Thousands more had become prisoners of war. But when the victory celebration finally came, our Eighth Air Force commander, in addressing his British hosts, said this: "We hope that after we are gone, you'll be happy we came."

The American Eagle Squadrons

In the early days of World War II, 244 American pilots made their way to England and volunteered to fly for the Royal Air Force. They played significant roles in the Battle of Britain during the months of August and September 1940, and subsequent action against the Luftwaffe.

In 1940 and 1941 three fighter squadrons were created within the RAF specifically for the Americans; these units became known as the American Eagle Squadrons. A number of Eagles became aces by shooting down five or more enemy planes. The RAF awarded 40 decorations to 31 Eagles. In 18 months of operations with the RAF, the Eagle pilots shot down more than 73 enemy aircraft. Each squadron at some point led in total scoring throughout the RAF for a given month.

In September 1942 the three Eagle units were formally transferred to the United States Army Air Forces, where they became part of the 4th Fighter Group of the 8th Air force.

The 4th, in turn, profiting from the combat experiences of the former Eagle pilots, eventually became the highest-scoring U.S. fighter group of World War II.

The Eagles individual and collective experiences have been chronicled in three books by Vern Haugland, a veteran Associated Press war correspondent and later AP's aviation/space editor. The first two books, "The Eagle Squadrons: Yanks in the RAF, 1940-1942" and "The Eagles' War: The Saga of the Eagle Squadron Pilots, 1940-1945" were published some decades ago. A third book, "Caged Eagles: Downed American Fighter Pilots, 1940-1945," was completed just before Mr. Haugland's death in 1984. It was not published until early 1992 when his widow, Tess, was successful in finding a publisher for all three books in a set. These three paperback books are published by TAB Books, Blue Ridge Summit, PA, 17294, and sold at many bookstores. In Canada they are available through McGraw-Hill Ryerson, 300 Water Street, Whitby, Ontario L1N 9B6.

On May 12, 1986, the Eagle Squadron Memorial was unveiled in London in Grosvenor Square, directly across from the statue of Franklin D. Roosevelt.

Author's note: You may recall earlier remarks regarding my first combat mission, to Brunswick. I found these comments, with no author or publication noted— "Rough is the title of the mission for today, May 19, 1944. We went to Brunswick, Germany for the second time this month, but it was much rougher this time. Our bombs were dropped on the southern part of the city, after making three bomb runs. I don't know who was leading us over that blasted place so many times, but I could have given him a big kick. The flak was something awful over the target. Fighters also attacked us. We were under attack for about an hour, but it seemed like days. They came in forty and fifty at a time."

Some Stats on WWII Era Aircraft Losses

Taken from THE TIN GOOSE, an information letter of the Aviation History Club, POB 940445, Doraville, GA 30340
Military aircraft losses, 1939-1945:
Germany, 95,000
U.S., 59,295
Japan, 49,485
Great Britain, 33,090
Australia, 7,160
Italy, 4,000
Canada, 2,389
France, 2,400
New Zealand, 684
India, 527

(Russian losses were extremely high, but unreported by the Soviet government.)

Also included in the article were ladder scale listing of numbers of aircraft produced. 16,188 B-24s, 12,677 B-17a, 9,846

B-25Js, 7,385 A-20s, 5,157 B-26Es, 3,000 B-29s, and 1,355 A-26 Invaders. From *Crosshairs* Dec. 1989

My Shortest Mission

John F. Fay, 466th

Standing behind the pilot and copilot, I looked out the window and saw the No. 2 engine and part of the wing on fire. I tapped the pilot on the shoulder and pointed to the flame. He immediately turned toward land and I started to crawl through the tunnel to the nose to get my chute. I was the navigator, and my chest pack was at the navigator's position in the nose... My position during takeoff was standing between the pilot and copilot, calling out the airspeeds.

After takeoff, I remained on the flight deck as we were heading out over the North Sea. It was only ten to fifteen minutes after takeoff that the fire was first noticed... It was February 17, 1945, and we set out on a mission to Magdeburg loaded with RDX bombs. I recall that before takeoff, the crew chief was working on the No. 2 engine until just before we started the engines, but no one envisioned the problems we would soon encounter... Robinson, the nose gunner, met me head on in the tunnel, dragging his chest pack. I prevailed on him to back up so I could get my chute, and we then started toward the waist because the camera hatch was a better bailout opportunity than the nose wheel hatch. Going past the flight deck we saw Eclov (radio operator) and Curly (engineer) attempting to buckle on their chute straps...

By this time, the situation was getting desperate because the wing was fully enveloped in flames and it was loaded with gasoline. Upon reaching the waist, three of the gunners waived goodbye and bailed out, although we were still over the North Sea and the bail out signal had not been given...

Robinson and I positioned ourselves at the camera hatch and waited for the bail-out signal as the plane started down. As we crossed the shoreline, the pilot gave the signal and Robinson and I bailed out at less than 1,000 feet. The bailout was witnessed by personnel at the British Air Sea Rescue field at Langham, where we landed. The plane crashed on the other side of the field, killing the pilot, copilot, engineer, radio operator, and an Italian POW on the ground. British planes and rescue boats immediately attempted to rescue the men in the water, but it was too late. Unfortunately, the three gunners who bailed out over the North Sea perished due to the temperature of the water, although they were equipped with Mae Wests. Robinson and I were the only survivors. The whole trip lasted no more than an hour—short mission indeed!

The "Liberalization" of the Soviet Air Forces

Reprinted from the 446th BG's "Beachbell Echo"

As Soviet forces proceeded westward, more and more American crews chose to land their damaged aircraft in Soviet-held territory. Saving these machines for the Soviet AF was not an easy task. Some aircraft were damaged or destroyed by anti-Soviet partisans. Some were robbed by Soviet soldiers of everything which could be sold, and even guarding the aircraft did not always help. So, many aircraft were useful only for spare parts.

The first task in adopting B-24s and B-17s to Soviet service was replacing white stars with red ones. It was decided that Soviet airmen could not fly in machines with naked girls and other things painted on them, so orders were issued to get rid of all nose art.

The Liberator was not liked by Soviet crews due to her low aerodynamics. With reduced engines the speed dropped quickly; take-off and landing were difficult. These reasons may explain why the only American aircraft crashed was a B-24 (#42-94800). This machine lost one engine at take-off and broke in two parts during emergency landing. All crew in the tail part perished.

In the beginning of October 1945, the 203rd Air Regiment had 21 B-24s in flying condition. The B-17s were used in the Soviet AF to the summer of 1947; the B-24s served longer due to their more durable engines. The main reason for a B-24 to be put out of service was lack of pneumatic parts for nose wheels. B-24s were used for crew training since they were the only type aircraft equipped with a nose wheel. The last Liberators in Soviet service could be found still in 1950...

This and That

"I do not choose to be a common man. It is my right to be uncommon if I can. I seek opportunity, not security. I do not wish to be a kept citizen, humbled and dulled by having the state look after me. I want to take the calculated risk, to dream and to build, to fail and to succeed. I refuse to barter incentive for a dole. I prefer the challenges of life to the guaranteed existence, the thrill of fulfillment to the stale calm of utopia. I will not trade freedom for beneficence, nor my dignity for a handout. I will never cower before any master nor bend to any threat. It is my heritage to stand erect, proud, and unafraid. To think and act for myself, enjoy the benefits of my creations, and to face the world boldly and say, "This I have done..."

When we lived in the small hamlet of McElroy, Montana in the 1920s, hobos would be riding in and on boxcars, vagrants. They were also associated with the IWW—Independent Workmen of the World. A song to or from them went "Halleluiah, I'm a bum, Halleluiah, bum again, Halleluiah, give us a handout, to revive us again."

And in Lignite, North Dakota during prohibition Lee Dellage was the local bootlegger. He would check into Canada, get a load of gallon cans of pure alcohol, and return by back roads, over railroad tracks, not at the border check points. When the Ford V-8s first came out, Lee bought one as it could outrun the border police. One day he came to town and the V-8 had bullet holes in the trunk, but he outran the border patrol. I remember that on dance nights a friend's father, a cousin of Lee, would sell beer bottles with a mixture of pure alcohol, warm water, butter (melted), and nutmeg for $1. I remember the taste and the result. Okay.

A truck driver stopped at a roadside diner for lunch, and ordered a cheeseburger, coffee, and a slice of apple pie. As he was about to eat, three motorcycles pulled up outside. The bikers came in, and one grabbed the trucker's cheeseburger and took a bite from it. The second one drank the coffee, and the third wolfed down the apple pie. The truck driver didn't say a word. He simply got up, paid the cashier, and left. One of the motorcyclists said, "He ain't much of a man, is he?"

"He's not much of a driver, either," the cashier replied. "He just backed his truck over three motorcycles."

The horse and mule live thirty years and never hear of wine or beers; The sheep and goat at twenty die without a taste of scotch or rye; The cow drinks water by the ton and by eighteen is mostly done; The dog at fifteen cashes in without the aid of rum or gin; in healthful milk the kitten soaks and then in twelve short years she croaks; The modest, sober, bone dry hen lays eggs for nogs, then dies at ten; But somehow we outlast them all on coffee, tea, and alcohol; Which proves it sure can't hurt you none, to have yourself a lot of fun.

Author's note: I clipped this out of The New York Times long ago, and trust that it's okay to print. We did have a Dr. Seuss book or two when our children were growing up. What a rhymer!

"New York—It's diploma season, and across America graduates' eyes glaze over during commencement perorations.

Theodor Seuss Geisel, who lives in La Jolla, California, likes to write—he is Dr. Seuss, the author of children's books—but he dislikes making speeches. When Lake Forest College gave him an honorary degree in 1977, he was asked to give a formal speech.

No, he said, I won't but I'll say a few words when you hand me the sheepskin. He indeed meant a few words. The appreciative audience gave him a standing ovation. Here's what he said: "My uncle ordered popovers from the restaurant's bill of fare. And, when they were served, he regarded them with a penetrating stare. Then he spoke great Words of Wisdom as he sat there on that chair: 'To eat these things', said my uncle, 'You must exercise great care. You may swallow down what's solid, but you must spit out the air!' And as you partake of the world's bill of fare, that's darned good advice to follow. Do a lot of spitting out the hot air, and be careful what you swallow."

Robert Frost—"You don't have to deserve your mother's love. You have to deserve your father's. He's more particular." Or—a mother's love is unconditional, a father's, conditional... In peace sons bury their fathers, but in war the fathers bury their sons. Croesus.

The following are messages as published in the Wall Street Journal by United Technologies Corporation, Hartford, Connecticut 06101. 1983.

WILL THE REAL YOU PLEASE STAND UP?

Submit to pressure from peers and you move down to their level. Speak up for your own beliefs and you invite them up to your level. If you move with the crowd, you'll get no further than the crowd. When 40 million people believe in a dumb idea, it's still a dumb idea. Simply swimming with the tide leaves you nowhere. So if you believe in something that's good, honest and bright – stand up for it. Maybe your peers will get smart and drift your way.

AIM SO HIGH YOU'LL NEVER BE BORED

The greatest waste of our natural resources is the number of people who never achieve their potential. Get out of that slow lane. Shift into that fast lane. If you think you can't, you won't. If you think you can, there's a good chance you will. Even making the effort will make you feel like a new person. Reputations are made by searching for things that can't be done and doing them. Aim low, boring. Aim high, soaring.

LITTLE THINGS

Most of us miss out on life's big prizes. The Pulitzer. The Nobel. Oscars. Tonys. Emmys. But we're all eligible for life's small pleasures. A pat on the back. A kiss behind the ear. A four-pound bass. A full moon. An empty parking space. A crackling fire. A great meal. A glorious sunset. Hot soup. Cold beer. Don't fret about copping life's grand awards. Enjoy its tiny delights. There are plenty for all of us.

DECISIONS, DECISIONS

Sometimes the decision to do nothing is wise. But you can't make a career of doing nothing.

Freddie Fulcrum weighed everything too carefully. He would say, "On the one hand...but then, on the other," and his arguments weighed out so evenly he never did anything. When Freddie died, they carved a big zero on his tombstone. If you decide to fish – fine. Or, if you decide to cut bait – fine. But if you decide to do nothing, you're not going to have fish for dinner.

DON'T QUIT

Is that what you want to do. Quit? Anybody can do that. Takes no talent. Takes no guts. It's exactly what your adversaries hope you will do. Get your facts straight. Know what you're talking about. And keep going. In the 1948 Presidential election, the nation's leading political reporters all predicted Harry Truman would lose. He won. Winston Churchill said, "Never give in."

"Never. Never." Sir Winston stuck his chin out and wouldn't quit. Try sticking out your chin. Don't give up. Ever.

DON'T BE AFRAID TO FAIL

You've failed many times, although you may not remember. You fell down the first time you tried to walk. You almost drowned the first time you tried to swim, didn't you? Did you hit the ball the first time you swung a bat? Heavy hitters, the ones who hit the most home runs, also strike out a lot. R. H. Macy failed seven times before his store in New York caught on. English novelist John Creasey got 753 rejection slips before he published 564 books. Babe Ruth struck out 1,330 times, but he also hit 714 home runs. Don't worry about failure. Worry about the chances you miss when you don't even try.

Two books I liked, *Sweet Agony II, a writing book of sorts*, by Gene Olson, about the fun and challenge of writing, but the frustration of trying to get it better, and *The Secret of Santa Vittoria*. It's a novel about Germans in WWII taking over this little Italian village, and to protect their wine, the villagers hid it in caves. Well, in December 1996 we're driving around northern Italy and here's a road sign "Santa Vittoria." So up and up we drive to this little hilltop village that does have caves. Stopping for a cappuccino, because we were fully addicted after a few days in Italy, and because a worker was not around, a chef called to do the honors. I mentioned we had not as yet had truffles. He took us to his large, beautiful restaurant kitchen and showed us a supply in his refrigerator. He gave us three. They were white, as opposed to the more highly prized black variety, and quite small. I had to strongly insist on a gratuity. So that night we mentioned this to our restaurant's owner, with the result of shaved truffles on our pasta. Great!

In Tribute to "Our Little Friends" Col. Hubert "Hub" Zemke

John L. Frisbee

Reprinted with permission from Air Force Magazine, *April 1995*

Col. Hub Zemke was one of the preeminent World War II fighter commanders in the European Theater. His 56th Fighter Group, the "Wolfpack", was credited with 665 air-to-air victories, leading all fighter groups in the European Theater of Operations. Zemke alone had 17.75 confirmed victories in 154 combat missions, putting him in the top twenty-five of all Army Forces World War II fighter pilots. He once said that if he had been a better shot, he would have had twice as many.

Zemke was a professional fighter pilot before the U.S. entered the war. His insistence on discipline in the air and on the ground earned him the respect of all his men, but not always the love of some high-spirited pilots. A superb tactician, he originated the Zemke Fan and other tactical innovations. The Zemke Fan drastically changed Eight Air Force policy that had required escorting fighters to stay with the bombers at all times. Colonel

Zemke was convinced that if some fighters fanned out well ahead of the bombers, many enemy fighters could be shot down as they were forming up to attack the bomber stream. Lt. Ben. William E. Kepner, who headed VIII Fighter Command, bought the idea. Bomber losses declined significantly as fighter victories increased.

The Zemke Fan was first tried on May 12, 1944. On that mission, Hub Zemke's element lost one of its four P-47s to an abort. The remaining three were attacked by seven Messerschmitt Bf-109s. Zemke immediately ordered them to form a Lufbery circle. The Luftwaffe leader cut across the circle, and in a dazzling display of deflection shooting, downed one P-47. A few moments later, he repeated his performance, leaving Zemke alone in an unfriendly sky. With no recourse, Zemke went into a barrel-rolling vertical dive at full throttle and escaped. (Years later, he learned that the German sharpshooter was Maj. Günther Rall, the Luftwaffe's third-ranking ace with 275 victories.)

A somewhat shaken Zemke headed for home, escaping another formation of Bf-109s en route. Near Koblenz, Germany, he saw many 109s forming up below. The aggressive spirit that had made him an outstanding college and semipro boxer took over. He contacted two members of the 56th FG who arrived as a number of 109s grew to thirty. Zemke told his men to fly top cover while he went down alone to take on the enemy fighters. He shot down one before his fuel ran low and he had to break off for home.

In August 1944, after commanding the 56th FG for two years, Zemke volunteered to take over the 479th Fighter Group, equipped with P-38 Lightnings but about to convert to P-51 Mustangs. The 479th's record had not been good. Zemke soon restored the group's morale while earning three more victories himself.

As October drew to a close and his combat hours passed 450, Zemke knew his days as a group commander were about to end. He was ordered to 65th Fighter Wing headquarters as chief of staff.

With his bags packed, he decided to fly one more mission before taking over a desk.

On that mission he ran into the worst turbulence he had ever encountered. He ordered his formation to turn back, but before he could do so, his P-51 lost a wing. Parachuting from the wreckage, Zemke was soon taken prisoner and ended up in Stalag Luft I at Bart, Germany, on the Baltic Sea.

Newly arrived, Colonel Zemke found himself senior officer in command of 7,000 Allied prisoners, some of whom had been there for several years. Conditions were deplorable: insufficient food, inadequate clothing and medical attention, a lack of military discipline among some POWs, and indifferent or hostile German officials.

Zemke quickly established his leadership of the POWs, who numbered about 9,000 by VE Day. Gradually he developed working relations with the prison commandant and staff and achieved some improvements in living conditions.

As it became apparent that their war was lost, the Germans became more cooperative, especially as Soviet armies approached from the east. Zemke and his staff negotiated an arrangement with the camp commandant for the Germans to depart quietly at night, bearing only small arms, and turn the camp over to the Allied POW wing.

To avoid conflict between some POWs and the hated guards, Zemke's staff kept the arrangement secret until the morning after the German departure. Zemke then nurtured friendly relations with the arriving Soviets. (In 1941, he had spent several months in the USSR teaching Russian pilots to fly the P-40. He spoke some Russian and fluent German.) Ultimately, Zemke arranged for the POWs to be flown to Allied territory. His strong leadership saved the lives of many POWs.

Col. Hub Zemke retired from the Air Force in 1966 and died

August 30, 1994, at Oroville, California. He was an extraordinary man, outspoken, courageous, and of unflagging personal integrity and conviction. These qualities, which made him one of our greatest wartime leaders, did not endear him to some of his military superiors and probably denied him the rank and responsibilities he deserved. Nevertheless, he will remain a symbol of military excellence long after others are forgotten.

Russian Excursion—World War II Style

As told to David Paterson by his 445th BG crew members

Reprinted from the 2ADA Journal.

The second evening we were there the base C.O., a Russian Colonel, had a party for us.

In addition to our crew of eight, there were about fifteen Russian AF officers. Our crew was all seated at the Colonel's end of the table. We were served a borscht-type soup, thick with vegetables, some strange fresh-cooked meat, black bread, and real butter. Empty water glasses were at each place; pitchers of water and "soda-pop" looking bottles of clear liquid were placed up and down the table. The Colonel poured his glass half full of the clear liquid, and filled up the glass with water. As everyone else in the room did the same, we obediently followed suit. The Colonel stood up. "Stalin, Roosevelt, Churchill!" All glasses were raised, and all went bottom up. Wow! Did that burn! The "pop" was pure 100% alcohol!

As the evening progressed, the Russians got delight and laughs at our incapability to keep up with their drinking. Toast after toast was proposed, with all possible combinations of Churchill, Roosevelt, Stalin, Zhukov, Eisenhower, Patton, etc. etc. etc.

After dinner we staggered, while the Russians walked, up the outside stairs into a big upstairs room. There, with the music being furnished by two or three of the group who played guitars and the like, a dancing party concluded the evening. The dancing was Cossack style, men with men partners. We were wheedled into joining, which created great merriment not only because we had no idea of the dance steps required but because of the vast quantities of vodka we had consumed.

The next few days gave us insight into several things. Despite our constant pleas to have our plight communicated to U.S. forces, it was obvious nothing was done in this regard. Emergency facilities were minimal at this base. We saw a Yak come in to land, tail too high. He hit the brakes, and finally skidded to a halt with the nose in the dirt, tail up in the air. From an old rickety shed across the field came the sound of someone trying to crank-start an engine. This failed, then several men pushed, by hand, out of the shed an old square-built ambulance, World War I vintage. With one-man steering, and three to four pushing, they pushed this "emergency vehicle" over to the wrecked plane. They dragged the pilot out, put him in the ambulance, and again hand-pushed it, this time to the hospital. Fortunately, the pilot was no worse than bruised and shaken up. We never saw any medical equipment in the "hospital." We assumed a few bandages and lots of vodka solved all problems.

One morning, after about a week of what was becoming more

and more obvious confinement, lo and behold a C-47 with U.S. markings circled the field, landed, and taxied up. ATC, the pilot said, made a practice of touring every week or so up and down these areas, looking for downed crews. They saw our B-24, and came in for us. Little more was said, we hurriedly got our stuff together and climbed aboard. We didn't wait to say goodbye to the Russians, because we weren't sure we'd get away if they got wind of our intended departure. (In all fairness to the Russians, they were a combat unit, flying daily combat from a few miles behind the front lines; they had more pressing matters to attend to than providing us with the immediate service we desired. But we weren't about to let this opportunity go!)

The C-47 took us to Poltava, Russia, a U.S. shuttle base. There we were washed, deloused, and issued clean Class B uniforms. We were issued orders marked "Secret" directing us to proceed by the best and most direct military means possible to the 8th AF HQ in England.

Our return trip was interesting. It included stops at Teheran, Cairo, Libya, Athens, Rome, Naples, Marseilles, Paris, and finally London, and then our base at Tibenham, all of this courtesy of U.S. Air Transport Command. Because of ATC flight schedules, we stayed over at several of these places, sometimes several days each and, whenever we had time, were able to sightsee by borrowed Jeep or tour vehicle, courtesy of the USAAF.

(Sightseeing in Paris, by the way, included such sights as all-night nightclubs, etc.!)…

Upon our return to our base at Tibenham, we first rescued our belongings (the items which hadn't mysteriously disappeared, that is!) from the MIA (missing in action) storage room, then got new quarters assignments, and reported for operational duty. We resumed bombing flights shortly thereafter, almost a month to the day of the Zossen raid.

Soldiers, Sailors and Airmen of the Allied Expeditionary Force

Eisenhower's D-Day Speech

You are about to embark upon the Great Crusade, toward which we have striven these many months. The eyes of the world are upon you. The hopes and prayers of liberty-loving people everywhere march with you. In company with our brave Allies and brothers-in-arms on other Fronts, you will bring about the destruction of the German war machine, the elimination of Nazi tyranny over the oppressed peoples of Europe, and security for ourselves in a free world.

Your task will not be an easy one. Your enemy is well trained, well equipped and battle-hardened. He will fight savagely.

But this is the year 1944! Much has happened since the Nazi triumphs of 1940-41. The United Nations have inflicted upon the Germans great defeats, in open battle, man-to-man. Our air offensive has seriously reduced their strength in the air and their capacity to wage war on the ground. Our Home Fronts have given us an overwhelming superiority in weapons and munitions of war, and placed at our disposal great reserves of trained fighting men. The tide has turned! The free men of the world are marching together to Victory.

I have full confidence in your courage, devotion to duty and skill in battle. We will accept nothing less than full victory!

Good luck! And let us beseech the blessing of Almighty God upon this great and noble undertaking.

–Dwight D. Eisenhower

OSS Code Name:

Carpetbagger

Jim Hanford

Reprinted from *Yankee Wings*

Liberators assigned to "Carpetbagger" operations had to be modified. The ball turret was removed, and in its location a metal-shrouded circular hatch, called a "Joe Hole," was provided for the agents to drop through. At just under sixteen tons, the Liberator was too heavy to land on the improvised landing strips in occupied Europe. The nose turret, if installed, was also removed. In its place a greenhouse provided a good view of the drop zone, and enabled the bombardier to assist the navigator in pilotage. Additional navigation equipment included the British radio navigation aid, GEE, a U.S. Navy homing system which was effective up to 100 miles; and a radar altimeter of extreme accuracy for use in making drops. Blister windows were installed to improve the pilot's visibility, and flame dampers were added to suppress engine exhaust flames. Waist guns were also removed, and black-out curtains covered the waist windows. Finally, the entire exterior was painted non-glare black. With the aircraft blacked out in flight, a "Carpetbagger" B-24 was practically undetectable at night.

All operations over enemy territory were conducted during total darkness. As a result, the crews of four officers and four airmen began briefings at 1:00 p.m. Afterward, the crews drew up their own flight plans. Routes normally consisted of dog-legs, no longer than 30 miles each, to avoid known anti-aircraft guns and to discourage interceptions by night fighters. At least ten minute intervals were allowed between planes entering the same area. Most offloading operations were coordinated with lights or fires on the ground. The final approach was made at slow speed and 400 feet altitude (600 feet if "Joes" were dropped).

Such missions were fraught with danger. One Liberator returned to Harrington with over 1,000 bullet holes, resulting from a tangle with two night fighters. On April 27, 1944, 1st Lt. George Ambrose was flying "The Worry Bird" on a mission over France. While pushing a package through the "Joe" hole Jim Monier, who was on his first "Carpetbagger" mission, slipped and tumbled through the opening. It is believed he rode the package parachute down, for although he was badly injured, he survived the fall, and the war, as a POW. The next night "The Worry Bird" was shot down with only two survivors... The "Carpetbaggers" dropped 100 three-man teams, composed of two officers and a radio operator, just prior to and after D-Day, and their effect was significant... During the period January to May 1944, 25 Liberators were lost on "Carpetbagger" operations, and another eight were so severely damaged by ground fire that they were scrapped. By the war's end, some 4,500 tons of material and hundreds of "Joes" had been dropped. There were other operations mounted with B-24s to assist the Underground in Scandinavia, but that is another story.

Recovery Team Gets First Glimpse of B-24 Crash Site in China

Xing'an, China (AP)

Jan. 14, 1997

The two farmers were nine hours by foot from the nearest village, searching for herbs on south China's tallest mountain, when they spotted an airplane wing jutting up from a cliff. It turned out to be the shreds of an American B-24 that crashed with a crew of ten men during World War II, missing for 52 years. U.S. officials from the POW/MIA office in Washington got their first chance Monday to examine remains and wreckage that local officials had retrieved from the crash site. The U.S. team was scheduled to hike to the crash site today. It is only the second time that remains of airmen missing from World War II have been recovered in China, said Jay Liotta, deputy director of the POW/MIA office and a member of the mission. The other recovery was from a glacier in Tibet in 1994.

The farmers in Guangxi, on the border with Vietnam, discovered the wreckage on Oct. 2nd. Within weeks, local officials mobilized 500 workers, including museum experts, to bring back human bones and parts of the plane. The U.S. officials found the remains carefully placed on a long table. Beside them were eye glasses in a case, the dog tags of five men, coins from India, two pocket watches, and a fountain pen. On the floor nearby were twisted chunks of the plane, some with the U.S. military star still visible.

Jiang Jun, 29, one of the farmers who found the wreckage, said he and his friend Pan Qiwen were looking for a path when they spotted the wing. After a steep climb of more than 3000 feet, they reached the wreckage scattered on a cliff. Jiang said he had never seen an airplane, except on television. The two immediately reported the find and will be rewarded with $6,000, a county official said.

The bomber lost on Mao'er mountain set out from Liuzhou on August 31st, 1944, and bombed Japanese ships around Taiwan. Warned by radio not to return to Liuzhou because Japanese bombers were attacking the base, it headed back in bad weather at night to Guilin. It crashed 990 feet below the summit of the 7,068-foot mountain.

Stevens and Holm—Ditching with Nose Turret Shot Off

B-17

391st BG

On June 20, 1944, Lt. Charles Sevens and his copilot, Lt. Bill Holm, did an outstanding job with their aircraft when they ditched their plane #42-95171 with the nose turret shot off. One flak burst had shot away the entire nose section, instantly killing the navigator, Lt. Harold R. Meng, and the bombardier, Lt. William F. Weck. The plane left the target with two engines out, and a third engine was lost over the English Channel. The remaining engine was losing power as they ditched just off Dover. Two other crew members parachuted and were lost. Bill Holm reported than an Englishman on shore was trying to wave him back into the water. When he finally made shore, the man told him: "You're lucky, Yank—the area's mined and a Typhoon pilot was blown to bits following your path yesterday."

Lt. Stevens returned to combat Nov. 26, 1944, only to be blown clear of his aircraft over Misburg. He finished the war in a POW camp. He remained in the Air Force after WWII and was killed flying fighters in the Korean War. Bill Holm, retired from NASA, continues to fly his own plane today.

On The Trail of "Wabbit Tracks"

On 6 March 1944 the 8th Air Force completed its first mission to Berlin amid heavy flak, fighters, and cloud cover up to 29,000 feet. A formation of 658 heavies took part in this raid, and 69 of the bombers didn't return—the highest number ever lost on a single day. The 458th dispatched twenty-seven B-24s for the sortie, and five failed to return. This would be their highest total of losses on any mission for the remainder of its tour.

One of the wounded 458th Libs that limped away from the German capital was #41-29286-T, better known as "Wabbit Tracks." Just over the Dutch border and approaching Amsterdam, the crew saw that their "bunny" could go no farther and bailed out. Capt. Jack Bogusch, the pilot, was killed on this mission. The ship crashed in a field and was demolished... In October, 1995, Robert Swift, the bombardier, and Robert Robinson, waist gunner, and his three sons visited the crash site of the ship at Tubbergen, Holland. With the help of a local historian and metal detectors, they located the exact spot of Wabbit Tracks' demise. They recovered small bits and pieces of the plane along with some .50 caliber ammo. The historian, Martin Klaassen, had salvaged a 36" x 14" section of a wing after the crash and gave it to Bob, who carried it home for mounting on the wall behind his easy chair.

Over the past 52 years, this is only the second known case of 458th crewmen going back to the site of their plane's crash. The other was when the late Richard Eselgroth, navigator, went to an area southeast of Frankfurt, Germany in 1974 and recovered parts of 44-10491, "The Iron Duke," shot down 22 Feb. 1945... George Reynolds (458th), 4009 Saddle Run Circle, Pelham, AL 35124.

Lest We Forget

Myron Keilman, 392nd BG

On 16 November 1943 eighteen B-24s of the 392nd took off on a nine-and-a-half-hour mission to bomb the Germany heavy water plant at Rjukan, Norway. Lt. Harold (Doc) Weiland was the lead bombardier. Major Lawrence Gilbert, our group operations officer, was the command pilot. At the time, none of us were aware of the strategic importance of heavy water (ordinary hydrogen replaced by an isotope of twice the atomic weight called deuterium) being used in the production of the first atomic bombs. The Norsk Hydro hydrogen electrolysis plant near Rjukan was the only plant available to the Germans capable of manufacturing heavy-water in significant quantity. The plant was a large six-story concrete and steel structure, situated like a fortress on a mountain cliff. British Intelligence, early in 1942, made Prime Minister Churchill aware of its strategic importance. On 18 Oct. 1942 and 18 Feb. 1943 small teams of British and Norwegian commandos parachuted into isolated areas. On 27 Feb. 1943 they linked up 18 miles from the plant. At midnight 28 February they performed one of the most daring raids ever, and destroyed the high concentration heavy-water tanks.

By midnight April 1943 the plant was repaired—and security

greatly   strengthened   against   further   sabotage. Consequently—with British and atomic bomb research and development trailing—Winston Churchill and President Roosevelt made the decision to launch a heavy bomber attack. On Nov. 1943 the Second and Third Divisions of the Eight Air Force struck the plant with 160 B-24s and B-17s. The heavy water plant was put out of commission—never to operate again. The salvaged heavy water was sabotaged en route to Germany.

Dr. Joseph Carter, Professor of Nuclear Engineering, University of Kentucky, having served in the research and development of the atomic bomb under General Leslie Groves of the Manhattan Project, stated in Nov. 1988, "The bomber run of 16 Nov. 1943 and the subsequent destruction of nuclear laboratories at Peenemünde was a major contribution to winning World War II."

Think! What would the world be like today had the Nazi Regime been able to perfect and deploy the atomic bomb?!

From BOMBER
LEGENDS—Dear
Editor

The Beacon, Nov. 25, 1998

In your September 1997 issue here was something that sent up the "red flag," and I was disturbed by it. You listed the names of World War II and Vietnam veterans who gave their lives for their country. What about Korea?

Korea is called "the forgotten war," but one cannot understand why. It was very much a war. I was there. I know that one Francis Eugene Holland was the first Eagle Rock casualty and there may be others. I believe you should honor the Korean War as a war and a tablet should be mounted on the wall of the auditorium with the others.

Here are some facts. 8,177 men are still missing in action. 389 men are still listed as prisoners of war. 54,262 of the military force did not make it back. Also, it should be noted, that in the three years, one month and two days of the Korean conflict almost as many men were lost as compared with the 58,202 who died in the Vietnam war, which lasted eleven years and nine months. Military historians now agree that Korea was one of the bloodiest wars in the history of this country.

Thank you for giving this letter your attention.

Sincerely, Don Sutherland

Impact of Air Combat

Carl H. Albright, 446th BG, Flixton-Bungay Update

Flight surgeons determined who was to fly and who was grounded. They voluntarily flew combat missions searching for answers to questions such as: What would be the psychological impact of aerial combat on young men in their teens and early twenties? How would they stand the rigors of attacks from the ground and air, flying five miles high? Would they be able to fire machine guns in subzero temperatures, with flak so heavy that some crews said: "It was so thick you could walk on it." How would they react to seeing a plane explode in a ball of flame and men jumping with chutes on fire? How would they react when their buddy's bed next to theirs was empty? A flight surgeon once invited medical officers to consider the role of the combat flyer. He asked them to consider if they could manage 130 controls, switches, levers, dials and gauges of a bomber cockpit from the comfort of their swivel chairs. The flight surgeon continued:

"Cut your office to the size of a five-foot cube—engulf it in the roar of four 1,000 horsepower engines—increase your height above the ground to four or five miles—reduce the atmospheric pressure by one-half to two-thirds, and lower the outside temperature 40 degrees to 50 degrees below zero. That will give you an idea of the normal conditions under which pilots, engineers, navigators and bombardiers must work out mathematical relations of engine revolutions, manifold and fuel pressure, aerodynamics, barometric pressure, wind drift, air speed, ground speed, position, direction and plane attitude. As a final touch to their picture of concentration, ADD THE FEAR OF DEATH."

You Just Gotta "Hand It" To This Guy!

Reprinted from Stars and Stripes, *May 19, 1944*
A B-17 Assigned to the B-17 391st BG

Without a parachute, Lt. Edward M. Gibbens, of Mountain Home, Idaho, hung precariously by one hand in the open belly of a bomber high over the Channel for almost five minutes, then pulled himself up to safety. Gibbens, bombardier on the Liberator named "Sweating It Out," fell out on the way home from a raid after "chopping" bombs off the damaged rack with a fire axe.

The bomber ran into terrific flak over a French airfield and was shot up so badly that the bombs wouldn't release. It had 87 holes in the framework, all four engines were damaged, and the hydraulic system was shot out, meaning no brakes and an inevitable explosion in the event of a crash landing. While the pilot, Lt. Robert T. Hall, of Wayne, IN, struggled to keep the plane up, Gibbens shed his parachute, took the fire axe, and squeezed into the narrow catwalk to knock the bombs loose. The first one burst the bomb bay doors wide.

Bracing himself against a 100 mile per hour gale, Gibbons knocked the rest free, one by one. As the last one came free, Gibbens slipped on the catwalk, slippery with hydraulic fluid. He grabbed the bomb rack with one hand, holding the axe in the other. One slip of his fingers meant he'd go hurtling thousands of feet to death in the Channel. Slowly, he pulled himself back up to where he could regain his footing. Realizing he'd accomplished the feat with just one hand, Gibbens first words were, "And I didn't lose the axe..." (Bombardiers weren't just the guys who let the bombs go. They were the armament officer and the above was one of their jobs. Doing it, no room on the narrow catwalk for your chest parachute, so if Gibbens let go, he was a goner. If this has to be done at altitude, it was necessary to have a carry-on oxygen supply. Freezing cold, breezy, terrible job. I was always very appreciative of Phil Goplen, our bombardier, who had the not infrequent task of getting rid of unreleased bombs Sometimes the bottom ones wouldn't release, usually with smaller bombs, and higher ones would, so there was a pileup.)

Pilot Dead, Two Others Injured, Nose Battered, B-24 Returns

Reprinted from Stars and Stripes, *27 Nov. 1944— 445th BG*
With the pilot dead, two other crew members injured, and its flight instruments useless, a Liberator returned safely from a mission over Misburg on November 26, 1944—quick thinking and teamwork doing the trick. Several minutes before bombs away, the formation was attacked by enemy fighters. Lt. Vincent Mazza, copilot from Naperville, Illinois, fought to keep the bomber from swerving into other bombers after the pilot, killed by a 20mm shell which penetrated his flak suit, slumped over the controls. A second wave of German fighters lobbed shells into the Lib's nose, shrapnel wounding Lt. John C. Christiansen, of Plymouth, Michigan, who was manning the nose guns. Lt. Leo J. Lewis, bombardier from Clayton, Missouri, also was hit. The bombs were

salvoed by the navigator, Lt. Frank W. Federici of Chicago, who remained at his post in the nose.

When the enemy fighters departed, S/Sgt. Eddie W. Goodgion, right waist gunner from Lubbock, Texas, and T/Sgt. Carl E. Bally, radio operator from Ashland, Ohio, came to the aid of the dazed bombardier, whose helmet and oxygen mask had been torn off.

T/Sgt. Herbert A. Krieg, engineer from Atlantic City, NJ went to the cockpit and pulled the dead pilot clear of the controls. Christiansen made his way back from the nose turret to the waist, where his wounded leg was treated by S/Sgt. Kenneth J. Brass, left waist gunner.

At the channel, Mazza left the formation and headed for England alone. His maps blown away by the terrific wind which swept through the gaping hole in the nose, Federici directed the copilot back to base by recalling landmarks along the way. The radio and interphone went dead, making communication with the ground and other planes impossible. The tail gunner, S/Sgt. Charles W. Bickett of New Richmond, Ohio, had been cut off from communication with other crew members. Neither altimeter nor air-speed indicator were functioning. Massa circled the field behind another B-24 to get his proper landing speed, Krieg behind him to handle the throttles. The landing was fast, but smooth. Some of the most dramatic reminiscences were about brushes with death. Bob recalled having been assigned a plane on one particular mission that had just had bulletproof glass installed in it. The planes they normally flew did not have this feature. As they were flying, a fragment from flak hit the windows directly beside the pilot's position. On returning to base, they found it lacked a fraction of an inch from coming all the way through the glass. Both Bob and Marty agreed that had there been regular glass on the plane that day, Bob would not be here to tell the story...

Author's note: WHEN I read this I said, hey, this is pretty close to my experience with the thick glass that was only installed when the plane went to the repair depot with damage not fixable at the base. In my case, recounted elsewhere, the flak did get through the glass, plus the metal frame of the glass, and hit me at an angle which would have had my heart in the way. All I received was a sore black and blue mark. Of course, my body was not as resilient as two panes of the thick glass plus the frame, so it was literally a life- saver. I still have the piece of flak with glass embedded, and elsewhere include my picture with the two shattered panes of glass.

Drama Over Cologne, 14 October 1944

On 14 Oct. 1944, B-24J, S/N 42-50864, "Jolly Roger," with a crew of ten was the lead plane of the 458th Bomb Group, 755th Squadron, to bomb marshalling yards at Cologne, Germany. Immediately after bombs away, "Jolly Roger" was hit by three bursts of flak, knocking out the #3 engine and injuring several crew members, the most severe was MC Miller who was struck by shrapnel in the head and face. Lt. Robert Ferrel and Lt. Ernest Sands pulled Lt. Miller from the nose turret and administered first aid. The "Jolly Roger" was on fire and going down. Pilot Lt. William Klusmeyer ordered everyone to bail out. Sands attached a line to Miller's parachute ripcord and pushed him out the camera hatch, immediately followed by S/Sgt. Joseph Pohler.

Lt. Sands left the ship via the nose wheel doors and pulled his ripcord after passing through several cloud layers. After landing, Lt. Sands hid himself in a depression till after dark, and then started walking west. The nine other crew members had been captured by German soldiers. Lt. Sands evaded capture for seven days but was caught and beaten by German civilians as he was trying to cross a river to get to Belgium. Sands ended up in Stalag Luft III and on January 27, 1945, was marched west during a blizzard, eventually ending up in Stalag VIIA at Moosburg in the spring of 1945. On April 29, 1945, an American tank burst through the front gate at Moosburg with a force led by General Patton. It was one day before Sands' 24th birthday.

Ernie Sands always wondered what had happened to MC Miller. The last he had seen him was when he had parachuted from the plane. Had he survived? Many years later, after the war, Ernie received a phone call—it was MC Miller. He had tracked Ernie down to thank him for helping save his life. Miller had survived after being treated by German doctors and had fully recovered in a POW camp.

Ernest Sands served as North Dakota's Lt. Governor from 1981 to 1984... (Noted elsewhere is mention of my cadet friend Donald Nutter who lived through the war as a pilot, and died in a National Guard plane crash when serving as governor of Montana.)

Author's note: Artist proofs of Drama over Cologne, signed by bombardier Ernest Sands, are available from Scott Nelson, 6705 CR 82, Solen, ND 58570, 701-597-3525, www.scottnelsonart.com.

8th Air Force

Nomads

Sgt. Earl Anderson, Yank Magazine Staff Correspondent

Reprinted from 3D Strategic Air Depot Association Newsletter *(First published in* Yank Magazine, *circa 1944).*

As the men of the Eighth Air Force started to pack for the long trek home or to the Pacific, many of the ground force men are probably reflecting that, being based in England, they really didn't see a lot of country. But there was one group that followed close behind the advancing armies and whose trails crisscrossed every part of four Continental countries, and then led into Germany. Their shop trucks rattled over the transport-cluttered roads of France, Belgium, Holland, Luxembourg and Germany, and often, following their map coordinates, the men left the main highways to come upon secluded regions where the sight of American GIs brought curious natives into the village street to see their "liberators."

These men made up the mobile crews of the Eighth Air Force Service Command on the Continent. In groups of ten, headed by a sergeant, they left their home bases for weeks at a time, either to repair or salvage Eighth Air Force planes that had been forced down on the Continent and were unable to reach any one of three emergency landing fields.

The mobile crews were part of the Continental operations of the 8th AFSC that sent back almost 1,300 bombers and fighters before V-E Day. Summing up the accomplishments, Col. J.M. McCullough, the C.O., said, "Prior to D-Day all planes that could not get back to England were either lost to the enemy or the English Channel. But since the first beachhead was secured, of 1,288 planes, valued at about $300,000,000, which were forced down in repairable condition, all but 67 were returned to England and made airworthy. Critical parts were also recovered from 422 unrepairable planes which crashed on the Continent."

The first man to reach France after D-Day was John R. Campbell. He was then a master sergeant, but later earned a field commission. Campbell flew into the beachhead on D-plus-11 to count the planes that were down and run a quick inspection on them to see if they could be repaired. The first group of men—13 of them landed seven days later with only hand tools, and, of course, field equipment and arms. They tackled the planes with what they had, and with what they could "beg, borrow, steal or invent." One month after D-Day, two B-17s and one P-47 took off from the landing strips in France and headed for the depots in England.

Then began the race to satisfy the insatiable demands from the United Kingdom for planes to keep the divisions at full strength, and for parts that could be used to repair the damaged planes that had made their way home.

The "13 men and a jeep" grew into a full-blown Strategic Air Depot, and three landing fields were established on the Continent, where pilots were briefed in land in an emergency. The mobile crews went after those ships which had to land quickly on any old spot.

The crews were stocked with 10-in-1 rations. Sometimes they lived on those. Sometimes they scrounged. Sometimes they put up with other outfits near the plane they were repairing. Inspectors went ahead of them, finding the planes, putting guards on them, and marking them for "salvage" or for "repair." The crew would pile into their 6 x 6 shop truck as soon as one job was done and head for the next one, maybe miles away. They became the nomads of the Eighth Air Force.

When the pressure was on, as it was for months following D-Day, they started work at the crack of dawn, and finished at night using flashlights. They had to know every plane in the Eighth Air Force. No man could specialize. They took on Lightnings, Thunderbolts, Mustangs, Libs and Forts as they came. Hangars to protect them from the winter blasts were an unknown luxury.

"During those months it seemed like there wasn't anything between us and the North Pole but a bush," one of them said. "We'd keep a five or ten gallon can of oil burning near the plane to de-numb our hands."

As our armies pushed the Germans back, the Service Command men followed in their wake, and their shop trucks were familiar sights to the men in the ground forces.

They tell a story about one crew working on a plane in the Ardennes in the latter part of December. "Where's the front?" they called to a couple of infantry Joes. The men came over and watched the mechanics for a moment, then replied, "The front! If you wait a couple of hours, it ought to be right here. Our outfit is regrouping a couple of miles further back."

Buzz Bombs: D-Day Was Too Late

Graham Heathcote, Associated Press

(The writer, a schoolboy at the time, was there when the German V-1s and V-2s began falling. These are his memories.)

LONDON—In the early morning darkness of June 13, 1944, we heard a noise different from anything we had known though five years of air battles and bombs.

A far off rumbling in the sky became louder and louder, turning into a roar that shook the house in Kent and filled the fields with shattering sound. With a deafening rattle, whatever it was passed low over the house. The reflections of a red flame climbed up the bedroom wall and across the ceiling. Then the roar became a rumbling again, dying away as the thing flew on in the direction of London. I lay in bed petrified! My mother ran into my room in her nightdress crying, "Graham, Graham, what is it?"

The government did not tell us immediately, but the assault of Hitler's secret weapon had begun with the V-1 flying bomb. Just one week earlier, the allies had invaded Normandy, giving us confidence that peace in the air would come. It did not happen. The third of the four LV-1s on that first night killed three people in London's Bethnal Green area. On September 8, another secret weapon arrived. The first supersonic rocket killed three people in Chiswick, west London. The V-2 was more terrifying because it could not be seen or detected.

In the closing months of World War II, Britain became the first nation to suffer attack by ballistic missiles from beyond its borders. The bombardment lasted nine months. The target was London, but the flying bombs and rockets fell all over southeast England, where American GIs waited to ship out to the continent. General Dwight D. Eisenhower, the supreme Allied commander, ordered more bombing of the launch sites in France and the Netherlands. By March 1945 when the attacks ended, 5,823 flying bombs and 1,054 rockets had fallen on England, killing 8,300 people badly wounding at least twice that number, destroying 23,000 homes and damaging many more. Another 2,771 people were killed in Belgium and France and 2,900 Allied airmen died in raids on launch sites and production plants. Both V-1 and V-2 were brilliant scientific and engineering achievements that might have enabled Germany to defeat Britain if they had come earlier. But after D-Day, they were militarily irrelevant.

Together, the flying bomb and the rocket created terror in London, which still bears scars from the attacks. One million people fled the capital to seek safety in the countryside. Another 250,000 mothers and children were evacuated by the government. Despite the terror, Britons managed a joke: they called the flying bombs "doodle bugs."

USAAF Air Transport Command

Excerpt from the Book Official Pictorial History of the USAAF:

The Army's great aerial transportation agency was the Air Transport Command. Whenever men, planes and supplies had to be delivered in a hurry or whenever there was no other means of getting them where they were needed, the Air Transport Command took on the job. Under wartime conditions transport or combat planes crossed the Atlantic on an average of one every thirteen minutes, the broader Pacific, every hour and a half; and, in one year, more than a billion pounds of high priority cargo, passengers, and mail were carried to war theaters around the globe.

The ATC began as the Air Corps Ferrying Command on May 29, 1941 with two officers, one civilian, a world map posted in a Washington office, and an assignment to assist in delivering military aircraft to the countries then fighting for democracy. Within a year, airfields, isolated stations, and lonely weather and communications outposts had been built on deserts, tropical islands, and arctic wastes. The first ferry delivery reached Montreal on June 9, 1941. The first transatlantic flight—from Washington to Prestwick—departed on July 1. A trip to Cairo was undertaken in September, followed by a round-the-world journey touching Washington, Prestwick, Moscow and Singapore. From the first contract in August 1941, fullest use was made of the skill and experience of the commercial airlines flying under contract to the War Department and dependent for control upon the ATC.

After America entered the war, many civilian transport pilots were commissioned as officers to ferry military aircraft. Experienced commercial airline executives donned uniforms to serve on the staff of veteran flyer Lt. Gen. Harold L. George, who had assumed command of the Ferrying Command on April 1, 1942.

By June 1942, ATC routes touched all six continents. Routes were inaugurated to Alaska in April 1942, and in June, when the ATC took its present name, B-17s were delivered on short notice to participate in the Battle of Midway, and personnel and munitions were rushed to Dutch harbor to check the Japanese in the Aleutians. In July the first plane landed at Ascension Island base on the South Atlantic route, P-38s were flown to the United Kingdom in August, and A-20s to North Africa with the U.S. landings in November. In December the ATC took over the route from Assam to China, flown since April 1942 by the 1st Ferrying Group of the Tenth Air Force.

By 1945 the ATC, with more than 20,000 members in uniform, was flying with clockwise regularity routes that were considered unflyable before the war. To supply the Fourteenth Air Force and the XX Bomber Command, it carried fuel, bombs, jeeps, five-ton trucks, and 12 ½-ton road scrapers over the towering Himalayas, achieving during July 1945 an average of one plane every 1.3 minutes over the Hump. By the war's end, ATC operated eleven divisions, delivering at airplane speed to every front the critically needed items on which global victory was to hinge.

B-47 Stratojet

Author's note: My B-24 bombardier, Phil Goplen of Zumbrota, Minnesota, was recalled after his WWII discharge, and subsequently spent a dozen years as navigator on a B-47 crew. He has interesting stories about the Cuban missile crisis and how the 47s were prepared to bomb Moscow... I communicated with and had personal contacts with four members of my crew over the years after the war. They are, sadly, all gone. I learned of the death of the Snyder twins of Baltimore through Ken's widow. I never could find the radio operator or ball turret gunner, or Phil, bombardier. But last year he contacted Pat Everson, historian par excellence for our 448th Bomb Group, who has tons of records, to ask about any information of his WWII crew. SO—that's eight of the ten accounted for. It was lonely until Phil and I connected. As far as we know, we're the last two...

The B-47 was the first pure jet strategic bomber whose many unique features included six jet engines; a two-engine, pylon-mounted pod under each wing near the fuselage; and a single-engine pod further outboard. The wings were attached high on the fuselage and swept 35 degrees. The design incorporated revolutionary bicycle-type, retractable main landing gear with single, two-wheel struts on the forward and aft fuselage. Outrigger wheels added lateral stability and retracted into the two-engine pod cowling. The B-47 was 107 feet long, 28 feet high at the tail, and had a wing-span of 116 feet. The crew consisted of an aircraft commander pilot, pilot, and navigator... With a maximum gross weight of about 225,000 pounds, it used rocket assist on takeoff. They carried 17,554 gallons of fuel, which included two drop-tanks, 1,700 gallons each. Maximum landing weight, 125,000 pounds. A tail chute was used to slow down the aircraft during landings.

Although heavier than the heaviest World War II bomber, the B-47 was designed to be a medium-range penetrator with approximately a 3,500 nautical mile range. This was not a problem in the early 1950s since forward basing was available in the United Kingdom, Spain, Morocco, Guam, and Alaska. In addition, the B-47 was equipped with an air refueling capability and, on several occasions, 36-hour missions were flown.

The aircraft's payload capacity was limited to 20,000 pounds internally. Since nuclear weapons were large in the early 1950s, the bomb bay was limited to one or two of high yield. This lack of payload capacity was compensated for by the large numbers of B-47s, which resulted in an acceptable overall weapon delivery capacity. By 1956, B-47 deployment reached its peak with over 1,300 assigned to SAC (Strategic Air Command). Subsequently, phase out of the B-47 took place in the 1960s. It coincided with the rapid buildup of ICBM and SLBM deployment by the U.S.

In summary, the B-47 was a technological innovation in bomber aircraft design with swept wings, jet engines, the ability to be air-refueled, and an operational envelope equal to the fighter aircraft of the early 1950s.

Some statistics: Takeoff ground run, at sea level, 10,400′, jet assisted, 7,350′, over 50′ obstacle, 12,000′, jet assisted, 8,800′. Maximum speed, 600 mph; combat speed, 557 mph at 38,500′, 435 mph, average. Rate of climb, Sea level, 1,850′ per minute, combat rate with maximum power, 4,350′ per minute. Combat radius, 2,050 nautical miles. Tail guns, two .20mm cannons in remote tail turret. (With near-fighter speed and a higher altitude ceiling they could only be successfully intercepted from the rear.)

Bits and Pieces of a Tour

Frank A. Reed, 448th

With the 50th anniversary of what went on back in the 8th, many of us naturally attempt to recall the times and events that we lived through. I have read many accounts in the *Journal* of those involved where they told in great detail what transpired on a particular eventful mission they flew. Although my crew flew a few that would make an interesting story, it is beyond me to do the same. First of all, I didn't keep a diary to refer to. Second, I flew my missions in the tail, and as a result I didn't always know what was going on in the waist, much less what transpired up front. Third, after fifty years, even if I had known all the facts to tell a good story, with Mr. Senility creeping in on me, I would be hard pressed to detail any one mission. I do recall, however, as many of the readers probably do, many varied and isolated events, both in and out of the plane, that pop into my mind, with no recollection of what transpired just prior to or after the event; such as:

Still being awake at 3 AM before my first mission when someone from operations came to wake me up.

My first mission, and knowing this was "for keeps" when I saw one of our group go down.

My first real fighter attack near Brunswick, when we lost three planes.

Taxiing out to the runway to take off and seeing the English civilian workers give us a "thumbs up" salute. I liked that.

Twice seeing a 24 in our formation, while flying through a heavy flak field, suddenly disappear in a large ball of fire.

Going to a movie on the base one night, when the lights dimmed and the credits came on, "starring Jimmy Stewart," then seeing a pilot get up and walk out, saying, "I've seen this one, and it's not a very good picture."

In formation over the North Sea, at some 18,000 feet, just before entering the continent—icing up and falling out of control, finally getting control at 1,000 feet.

The *night* we returned from a *day* mission and the Jerrys followed us back, in our formation—the Jerrys shooting at us, we at them, the British ack-ack shooting at both of us. Everybody shouting, being strafed while landing, etc., etc. God, what an ugly ending for a beautiful (?) day.

The time the plexiglass three inches above my head was shattered by flak.

Seeing a fellow tail gunner sailing right past me in his turret when it had been shot away from his plane during a fierce fighter attack.

The night on leave in London during the mini-blitz, staying at the Russell Square Hotel when the Jerrys came over and hit the hotel, setting it on fire with incendiary bombs.

Escorting a P-38, under our right wing, home from a mission after he had lost an engine and probably had other difficulties.

The time our pilot, during a five abreast head-on attack near

Tutow, caught a .303mm slug square in his chest, but survived because he was wearing two flak vests.

The time my left gun barrel was hit and left dangling at a 90-degree angle.

Seeing my copilot, flying next to us, shot down on his first mission after getting his own crew.

That memorable night at the Strand Palace Hotel—with Ann.

The only "make-up" mission I had with a strange crew, flying a new silver plane on its maiden flight to the Ruhr Valley, returning home with some 300 holes from flak and being dubbed thereafter "Patches."

Always the fear of running out of ammunition.

The time during a particular fierce fighter attack when we salvoed a load of fragmentation bombs on one of our own planes, which while doing severe evasive action, slid right under us.

Waking up in the middle of the night in our barracks and seeing the glow of half a dozen cigarettes in the dark.

The day after 19 missions (over which we had lost 55 planes) when we were told that since things were getting easier, we would no longer do 25 missions, but 30.

Seeing the three double bunks right next to me emptied three times by crews shot down.

Seeing our right waist gunner, who had left our crew after a falling-out with our pilot, bail out with his new crew on his first mission with them, over the heart of Berlin.

The time on our next-to-the-last mission when #3 engine blew, caught fire, and we dropped out of formation to return home alone across Germany and France.

During a fighter attack seeing a group member who had bailed out going down right past me with his chute on fire.

Seeing a fellow crew member, late in our tour and after a

particularly rough fighter attack, completely break down, never to fly again.

The best five days in almost a year, which I spent in England at a "flak shack" near Oxford where a cute little English girl would wake me up each morning in my big double bed with a tray of orange juice.

Yes, bits and pieces of the past that I will never forget.

Rommel: Leader of the Afrika Korps; Master of Mobile Warfare

Reprinted from Lincolnshire Military Preservation Society Magazine, Lincolnshire, England

Field Marshal Erwin Rommel (1891-1944) was one of the great generals of World War II, and his inspired leadership of his armored and mobile formations made him a legend in his lifetime, even among his enemies.

After serving in the First World War, he taught at the new infantry schools and in these inter-war years he caught the attention of Adolf Hitler. When war came in 1939, Rommel was commander of Hitler's personal headquarters. After the defeat of Poland, Hitler granted his request to be given command of a Panzer division.

The division that he took over was the 7th Panzer. As part of

Army Group A, it was allotted an important part in the strategy that had been devised to break through the allied defenses in the Ardennes in May of 1940.

After the defeat of France, Rommel was recognized as an outstanding exponent of "Blitzkrieg," but his orders when he took up his next command were to be on the defensive. This command was of the German forces that had been sent to North Africa to shore up the tottering armies of their Italian ally, which were headed for Suez and beyond before being badly mauled and defeated by the British.

In spite of his orders, Rommel decided to take the offensive. This was the first of a long series of attacks, launched on 31 March 1941. The British, however, would not give up the port of Tobruk, which was only taken finally in November. Shortly afterwards, General Claude Auchinleck ordered the newly named British 8th Army against the Germans in Operation Crusader. This time the Allies had more success.

The first six months of 1942 saw Rommel recover from the setback of Crusader and take the offensive again. The initial German victories in this new offensive were stunning. The Gazala battles defeated the 8th Army and then Tobruk fell again to the Axis forces. Rommel decided to push on again to Alexandria, hoping to defeat the British totally in North Africa. He managed to reach El Alamein, but there, stiffening British forces forced him to a halt. He attempted many times to advance further, but failed in his objectives.

Under its new commander, Lieutenant-General Bernard Law Montgomery, the 8th Army stood firm.

As the autumn wore on, the Allies in turn prepared their counter-offensive, opened by the Battle of Alamein in October/ November 1942. Rommel had supervised the construction of a very effective defensive position, and although numerically superior, the British forces found it hard to break; but eventually they did so, and the Afrika Korps began a long pull back. Meanwhile, the Allies had landed an Anglo-American Army in French North Africa and were soon advancing on Tunisia. The Axis forces in North Africa were soon inevitably squeezed to death, but nevertheless, Rommel fought an inspired retreat as he pulled back, eluding Montgomery's attempts to trap him and his much depleted army and at the same time giving the U.S. forces a bloody nose in Tunisia at the Kasserine Pass. Rommel left Africa before the final Axis defeat in May of 1943.

In January of 1944, Rommel was handed the command of Army Group B, in France, preparing to meet the expected Allied landings in northwest Europe. He ordered great effort to be put into improving all beach defenses. After the successful Normandy D-Day beach landings, however, he clearly realized that the German Army would eventually have to retreat in the face of the invading forces. He advised Hitler of this. Hitler refused and Rommel gave some support to the plotters who were planning to assassinate the Fuhrer. When the plot failed and Rommel's name was linked with the plotters, he was given the option of standing trial or taking his own life. He chose the latter. What marks Rommel above most high ranking German officers was his insistence that moral standards must be observed at all times, on and off the battlefield—towards prisoners and civilians especially. This combination is rare in any epoch.

Journal Editor Visits with "Hump" Fliers

Ray Pytel, editor of the 2ADA *Journal* was invited to a reunion to outline the procedures used in collecting funds for the Bronze B-24 exhibit at the U.S. Air Force Academy.

The China-Burma-India Hump Pilots and Crewmen Association held its 56th Annual Reunion August 21-26, 2001 in Washington, DC. The members of the Hump Fliers Association are considering a C-46 cargo replica for the Academy's Court of Honor. The Hump Fliers flew C-47's (also known as DC-3's), the Liberator Cargo Versions C-87's and C-109's, and the roomy Curtiss 'Commando' C-46.

The Association is composed of nearly 3,500 air crew members and support personnel who were engaged in the China-Burma-India Theater of Operations during WWII. A major portion of the flying provided the entire supplies for the American and Chinese Armies and Air Forces in China—the first time such a massive airlift was ever attempted. The November 19, 1945 issue of *TIME* magazine reported on page 26: "Unofficial estimates were that 3,000 Allied transport and tactical aircraft had been lost among those jagged peaks (Himalaya Mountains). But for this price, the U.S. had backed China, and U.S. units in China, with invaluable aid: 78,000 tons went over the Hump in the peak month of July." These downed aircraft made an "aluminum trail" over the "Hump," as the Himalayas were called. The terrible weather and rugged terrain posed constant danger as did the Japanese fighters and bombers.

A four-volume set of books, CHINA AIRLIFT—THE HUMP records a first-hand "history" of the CBI Theater during WWII and was compiled by the members. HPA placed two memorials to those who flew the "Hump." One is located at the Air Force Museum, Wright Patterson Air Force Base, Dayton, Ohio. The other was placed at the Air Force Academy in Colorado Springs. The Museum of Aviation, Warner-Robins Air Force Base, Warner-Robins, Georgia, houses an extensive exhibit of the China-Burma-India Theater, and displays for future generations what was accomplished by these veterans. A new C-17 P-62 #90062 was dedicated in June 2000 to the memory of the Hump Operation. This aircraft is presently stationed at McChord AFB, near Tacoma, Washington.

The Hump Operation was made necessary by the loss of the famed Burma Road to the Japanese early in the war. With no other access a bad situation in China became desperate. Loss of an important ally seemed imminent. The legendary Flying Tigers were the first to suffer, for without fuel, bombs and ammunitions these heroic volunteers were helpless. The Chinese National Airways Corporation (CNAC) did what it could to fill the gap flying pre-war, DC-2/DC-3 aircraft over the southern India-China route.

It was soon apparent that CNAC alone couldn't bear the burden. Chinese General Chiang Kai-shek finally convinced a harried U.S. War Department of the gravity of the situation. As a result, a few planes, crews and support personnel were sent to India to start an aerial bridge over the mighty Himalayas to China. Active enemy air opposition, primitive airfields and lack of navigational aids hindered the operation at every turn. But the worst obstacle was the weather, which was always a factor, either on the ground, in flight, or both. Little was written or said about the Hump during its operation, which gave rise to the CBI's reputation as "The Forgotten Theatre." Losses were as great as any other WWII air operation and higher than most.

Once established with sufficient manning and equipment, the airlift kept China in the war until victory was achieved. Many Humpsters were coincidently supporting ground forces in winning the battle of Burma. HPA members point with pride to today's awesome airlift forces as their descendants.

Let's Play Tag!!!

Clayton K. Gross, 355th FG

In a thousand flights, including 105 combat missions in my two fighter tours, I remember this one as vividly as any, and man, would I like to meet the pilot of the Liberator that day!

My crew chief, Smitty, came to our Ops office in the early dawn to tell me that "Live Bait" was back in commission with a new engine and needed "slow time." I scheduled the sixteen mission pilots and with their two spares, and saw them off with the group for a deep escort mission. Then after another coffee with the Ops gang, I leisurely proceeded to GQ-I and after a proper pre-flight, lifted it into the broken clouds over Boxted.

There are few things I would rather do than fly a beautiful fighter plane, but nothing more boring than flying it straight and level when it was capable of doing so much. I leveled off just below the 3500-foot ceiling and decided on a sightseeing tour. First, I went south to the Thames, then turned West toward the barrage balloon fields of London. Before long on that course, I found company in the form of a B-24 cruising at the same altitude and crossing my course, left to right. Since it looked like something to do, I banked right and pulled along his right side. I really didn't want to frighten the bomber crew, so I sat—oh, maybe 50 feet off his wing tip, throttling back a little to match air speed. I could clearly see pilot and copilot not frightened, but grinning ear to ear. They beckoned me in, and now I grinned—they were speaking my language.

I moved in tight—like ten feet—but they weren't satisfied. With more waving and what I thought might have been a mouthed word "coward," they asked for it! I tucked Live Bait in under the Lib wing, careful only that their #3 and #4 engines did not slice through my canopy. The copilots gave me the universal "OK—Alright!" sign, and I smiled—not ready for what happened next. That bomber broke hard left and up like a fighter who suddenly discovered a covey of 109's on his tail. Blessed with pretty good reflexes which I honed in two years of flying fighters, I tucked back in quickly after the initial move left me just slightly behind.

For the next five minutes I went for a ride following that guy in maneuvers I had **no** idea a B-24 could do! I knew several things for sure—they had to be empty and the pilot was no beginner! After five minutes or so, which left me in a fair sweat, they leveled off and, still grinning, waved me forward. I couldn't believe it, but he tucked in on me. Probably I could have lost him if I really wanted to, but I didn't. I took them through the rest of the maneuvers the Liberator tech manual said they couldn't do—and they did them! If I hadn't been having so much fun in the air, I would have wished to be on the ground to watch the show—unbelievable!

When I finally leveled out, my big friend was firmly on my wing, still grinning. He then motioned me to follow and, leading our tight formation, flew north for 15 minutes. We gradually started a letdown until I could see trees at our level from the corner of my eye. Then we skipped over the last tree patch and let down to ground level—down a runway I found was a B-24 base.

I mean, we beat that field up the full length of the runway and then chandelled left and up. I thought he would make a fighter approach and land from that position, but he leveled out again and signaled me to lead the same kind of buzz job. I sincerely hope he was the Group C.O. of that outfit because what we were doing was my favorite pastime, and one that notoriously had me in trouble in my 355th Fighter Squadron. I didn't want them to suffer the same fate. In the meantime, I had the reputation of all fighter aviation to uphold, so from a mile or so out, I got my wingman in position—silently wished him well because I needed my concentration and would not be watching out for him. I gave that field a pass that may well have set a USAAF record for buzz jobs in which the participants survived. I know I cut grass and raised dust, and in the pullout, my friend was still there as always. This time he did roll out, gave me a giant wing waggle and made an approach and landing that would have made any fighter pilot proud. After his landing I made one more pass—rocking wings in farewell.

If I knew the markings of that aircraft, I have long since forgotten them. If I knew which of the Liberator bases we beat up, I have forgotten that also, but I do know that everybody at that station was out to watch the show and someone must remember it.

Issy was a Hero

by the author

The following was sent to the Madison, WI newspaper somewhere around 1998. By the author.

"Whenever our local columnist Herb Caen would write a beautiful column detailing the wonderful things about this just-deceased person, I would privately lament that he should have written it so the subject could have enjoyed it. But here I am guilty of the same thing. Although I am not a writer, I do wish I had sent this to you a year ago. I was the pilot of a B-24 crew that flew 33 missions in the Eighth Air Force in England the summer of 1944. My engineer, who was the top non-com of this ten-person crew, was from Cross Plains, Wisconsin. He had a trucking business, and was a very good mechanic. He also had a wife and daughter, but even though his age would have excluded him from service, he joined because he knew he had skills that would contribute. Many years later my wife asked Issy's wife Adeline her reaction to this. Her response, "I was mad." Americans were never so undivided as during WWII. It was a far different general attitude than we have in today's divisive world. We who experienced it are glad for it.

Issy (Isidore) was assigned to my crew in Fresno, California, Christmas time, 1943. We got a full crew at Muroc Air Corps base in the Mojave Desert (now Edwards Air Force base) where we had combat training for three months prior to an overseas assignment. While at Muroc—because of his excellent capability—Issy was offered an instructor's position where he could have finished out the war in the safety of a domestic base. I had forgotten this, but years later on one of my trips when I visited him he told me that he came to me with this offer and what about it? I'm happy that I was mature enough to tell him that we would certainly hate to lose him on our crew, but I couldn't stand in his way to accepting such a good offer. True to form, Issy turned it down as he wanted to have more exciting experiences than a training base position. Lucky for us. I was the oldest member of the crew save Issy, who was eight years older, and his mechanical knowledge of engines, his more mature counsel than mine, his position as the top non-com of this young crew (19, 20, 21 year olds) was absolutely invaluable to our successful mission completion.

In 1957 my wife and I visited Cross Plains. Issy was in his garage, under an auto, and I peeked in under the open hood. He spied me and I'll never forget his response. "For Christ's sake!" That after a thirteen-year period, but after that we had several more visits with Issy and Adeline. His business grew and he became a very successful Jeep dealer, which his family continues to operate after Issy's death last year.

One more story. We were on a mission, heading home, and here comes a German fighter coming in at US at about 1 o'clock. I could look right down his gun barrel, winking away at us. Issy is in the top turret and I call to him "Get him, Issy!" And his two 50s open up, shaking our plane. The German decided that this was a good day for both him and us to survive, and broke away before either was damaged.

So that is a short story about a pilot's engineer—a brave,

resourceful, intelligent, nice man. And a hero—Isidore Buechner, born, raised, lived, and died in Cross Plains, Wisconsin.

Landing in "Neutral" Switzerland

Reprinted from Wisconsin Badger News

In WWII, most of the 166 U.S. aircraft that landed in Switzerland did so out of necessity. It was either that or risk a crash landing in occupied France, or worse, running out of fuel long before reaching English shores. Only about five to ten percent of the crews landed there deliberately to escape the rest of the war. A large number of Americans escaped from the Swiss internment camps and made their way back to England. Of the 1,740 internees and evadees, 947 tried to escape. Of these, 184 attempts failed and the airmen were sent to brutal prison camps that were worse than the Stalag Luft camps in Germany.

The first airmen to arrive in Switzerland did not land there. They had been shot down over France or Germany and managed to make their way across the Swiss border. These men were considered "evadees" rather than internees. According to Swiss laws dating back to medieval times, they were entitled to sanctuary and some were free to leave like tourists. They were kept in separate camps from the internees who landed or parachuted into Switzerland.

A popular saying at that time was, "The Swiss are working for the Germans six days a week and praying for the Allies on the seventh!" However, the alliance between Switzerland and Germany was mostly an economic one. Looking at it from another perspective, if the Swiss had not cooperated with Germany, they would most likely have been annexed and occupied by German forces. Probably 95% of the Swiss people were openly pro-Allies.

The first foreign aircraft to land in Switzerland was a Luftwaffe Dornier Do-17Z-3 on 21 April 1940. The crew mistook Basel-Birsfelden airfield for a German field and landed. They were interned by the Swiss, but were later released due to pressure from the German government.

Until the summer of 1942, all landings or crashes of foreign aircraft on Swiss soil were made by Axis planes. A number of Me-110s and He-111s were shot down by Swiss fighters and a number of Luftwaffe training aircraft landed in error. Some of the German crews were allowed to return to Germany.

The first landing of an Allied aircraft was made by a British Mosquito in August of 1942. The pilot and copilot were returning from a recon mission to Venice when an engine overheated and they were forced to land at Bern-Belp airfield. The two-man crew tried to destroy the plane, but they failed in the attempt. The aircraft was repaired by the Swiss and later saw service in the Swiss Air Force. Both pilot and copilot were returned to England and paired with two German pilots sent back to Germany.

The first U.S. aircraft to land on Swiss soil was a B-24D named "Death Dealer." It was from the 93rd Bomb Group and had taken part in a raid on the Messerschmitt factory at Weiner-Neustadt. The plane was set on fire and destroyed by the crew. In an almost unbelievable coincidence, the first B-24 to land in Sweden was also from the 93rd Bomb Group and it too was named "Death Dealer."

The first B-17 to put down in Switzerland was from the 100th Bomb Group. They crash landed with #3 feathered, #2 shot up with the prop wind milling and the landing gear up. They had just left Schweinfurt on 17 August 1943. The second B-17 to land was from the 390th Bomb Group and had also been on the Schweinfurt mission. They bellied in near Berne on the 17th with two engines shot out. The last arrival landed on 20 April 1945. It was a B-17G from the 15th Air Force.

Of the 166 U.S. aircraft that landed, 74 were B-17s and 82 were B-24s. The rest were fighters and recon aircraft. A record of 16 U.S. aircraft landed in one day on 18 March 1944. Twelve were B-24s and four were B-17s. Six of the twelve B-24s were from the 44th Bomb Group alone. Some landings were highly questionable, such as when a B-24D from the 93rd Bomb Group, a veteran of the famous Ploesti raid, landed at Dubendorf on 16 March 1944. The Swiss noted, "The aircraft was virtually undamaged and contained enough fuel to get them back to England."

From August to October of 1945, 30 B-17s and 41 B-24s were flown back to Burtonwood in the U.K. The rest were scrapped in Switzerland. Ironically, those that were flown to England arrived too late to be flown back to the U.S. and so were scrapped at Burtonwood. Other items, such as aircraft equipment, bombs, flight clothing, etc. were hauled out of Switzerland by trucks to Munich-Erding, Germany where they were destroyed or burned.

Lest We Forget: "The Black March"

John Frisbee & George Gudderly

Reprinted from AIR FORCE *Magazine, Vol. 80, No. 9, September 1997.*

This article by John Frisbee, co-authored by Col. George Gudderly, chronicles the Black March and its casualties. Col. Gudderly survived the march and went on to a successful career in the Air Force.

Instrumental in the effort to place a monument at the location of Luft IV, he regularly writes and lectures on the subject.

During the winter of 1944-45, 6,000 Air Force noncoms took part in an event of mass heroism that has been neglected by history. Most Americans know, in a general way, about the Bataan Death March that took place in the Philippines during April 1942. Few have even heard of an equally grim march of Allied POWs in Northern Germany, during the winter of 1945 (the most severe winter Europe had suffered in many years). The march started at Stalag Luft IV in German Pomerania (now part of Poland), a POW camp for U.S. and British aircrew men.

Early in 1945, as the Soviet forces continued to advance after their breakout at Leningrad, the Germans decided to evacuate Stalag Luft IV. Some 1500 of the POWs, who were not physically able to walk, were sent by train to Stalag Luft I...On February 6, with little notice, more than 6,000 U.S. and British airmen began a forced march to the west in subzero weather, for which they were not adequately clothed or shod.

Conditions on the march were shocking. There was a total lack of sanitary facilities. Coupled with that was a completely inadequate diet of about 700 calories per day, contrasted to the 3,500 provided by the U.S. military services. Red Cross food parcels added additional calories when and if the Germans decided to distribute them. As a result of the unsanitary conditions and a near starvation diet, disease became rampant; typhus fever spread by body lice, dysentery that was suffered in some degree by everyone, pneumonia, diphtheria, pellagra, and other diseases. A major problem was frostbite that in many cases resulted in the amputation of extremities. At night, the men slept on frozen ground or, where available, in barns or any other shelter that could be found.

The five Allied doctors on the march were provided almost no medicines or help by the Germans. Those doctors, and a British chaplain, stood high in the ranks of the many heroes of the march. After walking all day with frequent pauses to care for stragglers, they spent the night caring for the ill, and then marched again the next day. When no medication was available, their encouragement and good humor helped many a man who was on the verge of giving up.

Acts of heroism were virtually universal. The stronger helped the weaker. Those fortunate enough to have a coat shared it with others. Sometimes the Germans provided farm wagons for those unable to walk. There seldom were horses available, so teams of POWs pulled the wagons through the snow. Capt. (Dr.) Caplan, in his testimony to the War Crimes Commission, described it was "a domain of heroes."

The range of talents and experience among the men was almost unlimited. Those with medical experience helped the doctors. Others proved to be talented traders, swapping the contents of Red Cross parcels with local civilians for eggs and other food. The price for being caught at this was instant death on both sides of the deal. A few less Nazified guards could be bribed with cigarettes to round up small amounts of local food.

In a few instances, when Allied air attacks killed a cow or horse in the fields, the animal was butchered expertly to supplement the meager rations. In every way possible, the men took care of each other in an almost universal display of compassion. Accounts of personal heroism are legend.

Because of war damage, the inadequacy of the roads, and the flow of battle, not all the POWs followed the same route west. It became a meandering passage over the northern part of Germany. As winter grew to a close, suffering from the cold abated. When the sound of Allied artillery grew closer, the German guards were less harsh in their treatment of POWs.

The march finally came to an end when the main element of the column encountered Allied forces east of Hamburg on May 2, 1945. They had covered more than 600 miles in 87 never-to-be-forgotten days. Of those who started on the march, about 1,500 perished from disease, starvation, or at the hands of German guards while attempting to escape. In terms of percentage of mortality, it comes very close to the Bataan Death March. The heroism of these men stands as a legacy to Air Force crewmen and deserves to be recognized.

In 1992, the American survivors of the march funded and dedicated a memorial at the former site of Stalag Luft IV in Poland, the starting place of a march that is an important part of Air

Force history. It should be widely recognized and its many heroes honored for their valor.

Excerpt from Chris Christiansen's book: Seven Years Among Prisoners of War; *Ohio University Press, Athens, Ohio (1944):*

As early as March 1944, the camp commandants had received instructions that in case of imminent invasion all POWs were to be evacuated from the border areas and the invasion zones. From September 1944 onward this evacuation claimed an incredible number of victims. And the closer the Allied armed forces came to the German borders, the more chaotic and undisciplined was the evacuation. I do not know just how many Allied POWs were killed in the process, but the number of British and Americans alone might be an indication; during the period from September 1944 through January 1945, the evacuations had claimed 1,987 victims, but during the last three months of the war that number increased to a total of 8,438. With so many dead among those who were relatively well treated and who—much more importantly, received Red Cross parcels with food for their daily meals, it can be assumed that the number of dead among the Russian POWs must have been considerably higher. About one hundred thousand POWS from the camps in Silesia were evacuated and marched through Saxony to Bavaria and Austria. Transportation by train had been planned, but had proved impossible because of the rapid Russian advance. Lack of winter clothes, food and quarters claimed many victims. Over-excited party members and nervous home guard (members of the "Volkssturm") decided the fate of the POWs in these last weeks of the war. The German High Command wanted to keep the POWs at any cost, to be able to negotiate more favorable peace terms, and it was therefore necessary to evacuate them under these most inhumane conditions instead of just leaving them to await the advancing Allied armies.

The Tempelhof Experience 1949-1951

William E. Hendrix, Jr. (466th)

Author's note: After a tour of combat with the 466th BG in 1944-45, Major Hendrix stayed in the Air Force and ended up flying C-54s in the Berlin Airlift. These are his recollections of that Cold War episode.

THE NORTHERN LIGHTS

Night missions on the Berlin Airlift were particularly difficult and nerve-wracking. We never knew what to expect in the darkness. (Barrage balloons trailing 1,000 feet long steel cables were a Soviet favorite. The steel cables would saw into our aluminum wings—possibly causing us to crash.) Light was usually non-existent except for the "black" light on the aircraft instrument panel. This night in January 1949—our first encounter with the Aurora Borealis—was a new experience.

The Aurora was low in the northern sky and widespread across the horizon. It hung in the sky like icicles but was irregular in size and shape. Adding to the eeriness of the Aurora was Saint Elmo's fire! Comparatively dim greenish yellow static electricity "played" along the top of the instrument panel and the outer edges of the windshield. Large halos of fire were formed in the arcs around the tips of the propeller blades. Fascinating! We saw the Aurora "fires" many times during the winter nights. Thankfully, they were harmless, but sometimes caused static electricity, together with minor shocks and noisy static in our radios.

THE BLUE LIGHT SPECIAL

Most of our landings and takeoffs on the Berlin Airlift were to the west. On this day, however, the GCA controllers had us landing to the east at the airfield (Tempelhof) in Berlin. This route placed us very low over a large rail yard just prior to touchdown. At the western edge of Tempelhof runway was a concrete wall about 8 feet high and 100 feet from the end of the runway. The top of this wall was the rail yard, about 100 yards wide to the west. Situated in the approximate center of the yard was a "farm style" blue light mounted on top of a 50-foot high telephone pole. I was the copilot on this trip. The pilot was my roommate and good friend Jack Thornton. Jack was a tall, lanky Texan (Denis, TX) and a superb pilot. As usual, the fog was thick and low. According to the rules, if we could not see the runway when we were down to 200 feet altitude, we were to abort the landing and return to our home base (Rhein-Main). We are now on the final approach to landing. We had already passed 200 feet—now down to about 100 feet and thinking of aborting the landing. Suddenly, from the dirty, gray "soup" came a quick glimpse of a bright blue light. I yelled to Jack, "Keep going, I know where we are!" Within seconds, the runway became visible straight in front of us. We were now down to less than 50 feet. We landed without incident and unloaded ten tons of cargo (food, flour, coal, etc.) for Berlin. To my knowledge, we were the only aircraft to land in Berlin that day—all because of a blue light on top of a telephone pole. Also, I was recently informed that as of February 1999, the blue light is still there.

Apparently it is there to provide light for the rail yard during darkness. On this day, it lighted our path into Tempelhof Airfield.

THE FOG UND SMOG CLUB

The 1807th Army Airways Communications Service (AACS) issued a 2.5 x 4-inch card for membership into the Fog Und Smoggers by use of the GCA controllers and was coveted by Berlin Airlift pilots. My tour of 125 missions on the airlift contained some 60-65 GCA landings. These were landings in heavy, dense fog which could *not* have been made without the ground controllers guiding us in by use of radar. The Berlin Airlift itself would have been impossible without the talent of the controllers and their radar—which was in its infancy! Yet, never once in all my GCA landings was I given erroneous guidance. On 12 January 1949, I was approaching Rhein-Main on completion of a mission to Berlin. As usual, the clouds and fog were thick and dangerous. After the landing, I was awarded a card which read 400 feet, visibility 2.5 miles. These measurements were incorrect because regulations would have been broken otherwise. The actual numbers were ceiling 75 feet, visibility 1/16th mile (528 feet). Looking back today, I think they should have been ceiling 25-30 feet, visibility 100 feet. Even then, I could only see the runway by looking down, not ahead. Landing was without incident thanks to the GCA controllers. However, I had difficulty seeing where to taxi to the parking area. This one was great fun!

PLAYING IN THE SAND

The runways at Tempelhof Airfield were built for German ME-109 fighters. No one ever dreamed that one day they would have to bear the weight and impact of four engine aircraft of almost *35 tons*. It wasn't very long before the most used runway was pounded into rubble. Someone came up with the idea to cover the runway with *sand* while another was being built. The sand was available in large quantity from several large lakes around Berlin.

The sand was trucked into the airfield and spread over the west runway to a depth of one foot. This made an excellent landing pad for a very soft touchdown which required almost no braking to stop the aircraft. It was generally necessary to apply power to get off the runway. Needless to say, the C-54s left deep ruts in the sand when landing. Solving this problem was a stroke of genius! Hundreds of Germans and displaced persons had made their way into the Allied zone (American) and could be utilized for labor. So, numerous persons were dispersed along both sides of the runway and provided with shovels, rakes or brooms. As soon as a landing aircraft passed by, they would swarm onto the runway and smooth out the ruts! They had to work swiftly because there was always another aircraft just about to touch down. Believe it or not, this worked quite well for some time. New runways were built in short order, and the Airlift wasn't even slowed down.

A HAIL OF A DEAL

On a flight out of Tempelhof to Rhein-Main this particular day, we are in the western corridor toward Hamburg. As usual, high, thick clouds and bad visibility. We began running into rain which soon turned into hail—lots of hail. The noise of the hail striking the aircraft windshield was absolutely *deafening*, even with headsets tightly covering both ears. Airspeed was usually 170 mph, but because of the hail I slowed to 150 for about three minutes. (Interval today was five minutes because of weather.) Shortly, I began to break out of the weather and resumed 170 mph. At about the same time I spotted what appeared to be a British C-47, according to the markings on the fuselage. It seemed to me that something wasn't quite right with the aircraft. Suddenly, I realized that there was a *jet engine* exhaust nozzle protruding from the bottom of the fuselage! I overcame the C-47 fairly rapidly and got a good look when—whoosh—it pulled away from me in short order. The pilot also dropped down into the clouds and it was gone. To this day, I have no idea what that bird really was or what country it belonged to. My main concern now was what damage the hail might have done to the aircraft. Good fortune was ours, and in spite of extreme noise, there was no visible damage. It was the worst hail I have ever encountered.

Reflections on
Tonopah Lights and
Delights

George A. Reynolds, 458th

Tonopah, Nevada, a small town near the California border, population 1600, was a training base for the 458th Bomb Group from about September 1943 to early January 1944. Based on clippings sent to me by historian Allen Metscher, it's apparent that the troops left this area—rich in history—to make some of their own with the Mighty Eighth thousands of miles away. A cartoon included in the clippings shows a milepost with distances to other places from the TAAF, and it tells quite a story in itself. It reads: Ely 176, Tonopah 7, Reno 240, Las Vegas 210, and Hell 0 .

Perhaps the last minute reading alludes in part to Metscher's research of the area since 1986. He has documented at least 26 crashes of B-24s and 110 deaths, and from the crash sites he still retrieves dog tags, engines, bombs, machine guns, gauges, wheels, and the like. He and other volunteers for the Central Nevada Museum have erected twelve markers at the crash sites, and they will complete work on the remainder as time allows. Surviving air crews labeled the base as decidedly jinxed!

There are, however, *some* pleasant memories relating to TAAF for those who served there, albeit living in tent cities while tussling with Army life at the time. Wong's cafe, featuring American/Chinese dishes, was a popular pit stop for the troops. Check these menu prices, with the trimmings: T-bone steak $1.50, sirloin $1.20, coffee or tea .10, chow mein $1.00, and chop suey .75.

The base opened in July, 1942, and pilots were training to fly the Bell P-39 Airacobra. But there were so many crashes that the fighter jocks moved out, and then came the Libs. It continued as a training field until closing in August '45. The airport still serves Tonopah-Goldfield, but little remains of TAAF.

The most prominent landmark in Tonopah was the five-story Mizpah Hotel. It's now ninety years old, and has hosted many celebrities over the years. Jack Dempsey was a barkeep and bouncer there before he found his niche in the boxing ring. Lawman-gunslinger Wyatt Earp stayed there quite regularly while chasing claim jumpers in nearby Goldfield. Howard Hughes married actress Jean Peters at the Mizpah. Kay Kyser, his band and gorgeous Georgia Carroll were guests while entertaining the TAAF troops. Finally, it is said that a lady of the evening was decapitated inside during the '40s and her ghost still haunts the facility.

The name Mizpah itself is rather intriguing. This Hebrew word, in an area known mostly for Indian folklore, was taken from the Bible's Old Testament in asking God to keep watch over travelers. Perhaps this is why Col. Valain R. Woodward chose it as a nickname for his B-24 when he left TAAF and joined the 458th at Horsham St. Faith. History confirms that it was a wise choice. Col. Woodward completed 25 missions, then was reassigned to HQ and eventually rotated to the States. Later he returned to the 458th and flew 35 more missions as C.O. of the 755th lead crew squadron until the war's end. "Mizpah," under the expert care of M/Sgt. John Miligan, completed 70 missions without ever failing to be ready when called upon, and then returned to the... ZI in June '45.

One of the local prodigies was Taxscine Ornelas, the owner of a bar frequented by TAAF airmen, and she became endeared to all of her customers. It was said that she never refused anyone in financial need and regularly collected small donations from the patrons in a "kitty" jug placed on the bar. These funds were used for various causes such as aiding the school in buying a badly needed bus, the cancer society, the Red Cross, et al. She also included the TAAF stockade, and the tenants said of "the Little Desert Mother," "If everyone had the kind of heart you do, this would be a different world to live in."

Taxscine died in 1954 at age 54 of a hemorrhage, but some say it was more likely a broken heart. A lady of the evening, her friend and a fixture in the bar, was murdered and the killer never apprehended. Authorities then closed Taxscine's bar and wouldn't allow it to reopen. She went into seclusion thereafter and died all alone.

Col. Woodward flew back to Tonopah in December '96. The flight was a birthday gift from his brother, and it would be interesting to have a recap of his memories after 50+ years. From several others who were stationed there, the comments are usually, "Most of us don't want to remember Tonopah—the cold, heat, isolation and wind. But there is one thing for sure—if you were there in 1943, you can't ever forget it!" The Central Nevada Historical Society is trying very hard to ensure that very thing. They continue to build their museum with artifacts from the war years as well as marking crash and historical sites, mostly with individuals' own time, efforts and funds...

Editor's note: In the late 1930s and early 40s, Lucky Strike cigarettes had an ad, LSMFT, translated as "Lucky Strike Means Fine Tobacco." Air crews about to be deployed to training bases had a different translation—"Lord, save me from Tonopah."

Chivalry in
Adversity
General Andy Low

Graduates of Service Academies have, for more than one hundred and fifty years, worn finger rings to commemorate their alma mater. In earlier years, before the advent of a gummed envelope, these commemorative rings served the useful purpose of imprinting the sealing wax on letters—even serving as an exterior identifier of the author. Many collegians of other institutions did a similar rite of passage. However, many of these collegians owed a closer allegiance to Greek-letter fraternities to which they belonged. Often their rings reflected this latter allegiance.

Since 1897, rings of West Point have reflected on the motto "Duty, Honor, Country" and the Academy Crest on one side of the ring, and a class-adopted crest on the other. During the third year, great activity by each class member marks the arrival of class rings.

Because of the closeness of the Academy experience—living in barracks, meals in a common mess, formations for all phases of daily life—the class ring is a ready manifestation of this closeness.

Most graduates wear their rings much of the time—and certainly at activities associated with the Academy experience.

And thus, I was one who wore my class ring most of the time. In combat, in Europe, in early 1944, we were required to wear our issue name plates ("dog tags") at all times, but were discouraged from carrying other identification which might be "of aid and/or comfort to the enemy."

On 31 July 1944, there was some confusion on the assignment from our Group for the Combat Air Commander. He would command the Second Combat Wing, and the Second Air Division, which the Wing would lead. As Group Operations Officer, I had been up all night during mission preparations, and thus was most familiar with targeting, routes, communications, and the myriad of detail to get over four hundred Liberator bombers to the target—Ludwigshafen, and the IG Farben Chemical Works. So, I took the assignment.

In a last minute rush, I changed into my flying gear and proceeded by jeep to Wing headquarters, some ten miles down the road.

Briefing, take-off, form-up, coast-out, tight formation—all went well until we began our bombing run. We were at 24,000 feet, the highest I had ever flown on an attack. We encountered heavy flak at our altitude, and took random hits with no personnel injuries up to "Bomb Doors Open." Just as the bombardier announced "Bombs Away" we took a burst just under our bomb-bay which set our hydraulic lines and reservoir on fire—a raging fire.

The crew fought the fire but warned we were in serious condition, with a chance of an explosion of the gasoline tanks above the bomb bay.

Quickly, the aircraft commander and I decided we had to leave the formation, dive to attempt to blow out the fire—and to clear the target area. I told the Deputy to take over the formation and we dove sharply in a sweeping arc away from the target.

The Flight Engineer in the bomb-bay reported that the structure was catching fire. We knew we had to jump, and the aircraft commander sounded the "Stand-by to bail" on the alarm, and "Jump" almost immediately.

We were three on the flight deck, the Pathfinder Navigator, the Aircraft Commander, and me. The Navigator attempted to open our normal egress through the bomb-bay. The fire was just too much of a blazing inferno. I had shed my harness, and stood up as he was re-closing the door. Over my head was a hatch used on the ground during taxiing, but was not an authorized egress in the air. It was forward of the top turret, and could be blocked by guns. It was forward of the propellers—but both number two and number three engines had been feathered. There were two vertical stabilizers on the B-24J, but we found out we had already lost one in the dive.

I bent down, grabbed the Navigator around his legs, and shoved him through the hatch. I followed quickly, and the Aircraft Commander was right behind me. We cleared the aircraft, pulled our ripcords—and the plane blew up.

I was alone as I floated out of the clouds close to the ground, and could see I was headed for farm land outside a village. As I neared the ground and prepared to land, I realized I was headed right at two military figures with rifles—and the longest fixed bayonets I had ever seen.

I touched down, collapsed my chute, and the German soldiers were not twenty yards from me, rifles at ready.

"Haben sie pistole?"

I did not understand what they said, but guessed. I shook my head and raised my arms, and then I realized I was really hurt. My flying suit was still smoldering. The Germans put down their guns and helped me beat out the embers. That done, they picked up their rifles, and began to search me. I was told to take off my watch by their motions. Then they emptied my pockets, found my dog tags but did not take them, and then helped me pull off my burned gloves.

And there it was—my West Point 1942 Class Ring. They motioned me to take it off, and it was dropped into a pack one soldier carried.

As they motioned me to march, I suddenly realized how scared I really was—and fearful of what was going to happen next.

We were taken to the village jail—all nine of us who made the jump. Two crewmen in the rear of the aircraft did not get out. We had all been quickly rounded up by the militia-type soldiers who had been turned out to look for downed men.

From the civilian jail, we were taken to a German Air Force airfield. We were given some medical treatment, wrapped with paper bandages, and readied for a trip to the Interrogation Center.

At the Interrogation Center, I was put in a plain, small solitary cell. I had told them my name, my rank and my serial number. I was bandaged so that I had to have someone feed me, and help with trips to the personal facilities.

My first session with the Interrogator was brief. I repeated my name, my rank, and my serial number. He called me major, but said he needed to know more. As he remarked, they did not give medical treatment to spies. I hurt terribly, and was not sure what was happening under the bandages. But, I had endured West Point, and I knew they weren't going to be any tougher.

The second morning was a repeat, giving only name, rank, and serial number, and back I was sent to my cell. Still hurting.

As I thought over my situation, and what was happening to the others whom I had not seen, I realized I had been riding with a 458th Bomb Group aircrew, transferred to the 389th as a lead crew. The aircraft wreckage would have 389th insignia. I deduced therefore they were not too sure who I was.

The third day session was another repeat. But the interrogator said I was foolish, as they would find me out. No medical treatment until they did. Back to my cell.

It was a warm August evening, but from my cell I could see nothing, and hear very little. Time dragged.

Suddenly, the guard was opening my cell, and in came a German flying officer. His left arm was mangled, and heavily bandaged. The guard locked him in, and went away.

In excellent English, with a British accent, he asked if I wanted a cigarette. I told him I did not smoke, so that ended that entrée. I really hurt and the bandage reeked, so I was angry enough to be rude.

He asked if I would like something to read—*Life*, maybe. I replied I could not handle a book with my bandages.

He said he was sorry for me as an airplane pilot, for me the war was over. But he added he would never fly again either. We warmed to each other—a little.

He asked about my family.

I told him I had a daughter I had never seen. He told me about his family. There was more small talk, and then he arose to leave. He walked to the door, and then came back to me. His good hand was in his pocket. He pulled it out and dropped my Class Ring inside my clothes.

Simply he said, "I am sure this means something to you, and it means nothing to them. Hide it, and do not wear it until you are free!"

With that, he turned quickly and left me alone—with my thoughts.

Can there be such chivalry among such obvious adversity? For me, there was.

How Did My Brother Die?

The story begins in England, on the misty morning of Wednesday, September 27, 1944. The 8th U.S. Army Air Force left its bases for targets in central Germany. Copilot Newell Brainard's 445th Bomb Group was assigned to the Henschel locomotive factory in Kassel, which was believed to be building tanks and cannons.

At the point where the groups split into separate bombing runs, amid cloudy skies and poor visibility, the leader of the 445th deviated 30 degrees from his route.

"That Mickey man (the radar navigator) in the lead ship has screwed up," one navigator said over his intercom. "We shouldn't have turned yet."

In moments, the planes were separated from the other bombers—and their protective fighter escorts.

The bombers of the 445th mistakenly flew to the town of Gottingen and dropped their bombs with no casualties or significant damage. Then the lumbering, vulnerable bombers followed the planned route back—50 miles behind the other planes, which had made a successful raid on Kassel. Veterans say the leader may have actually thought he was still on course and had bombed Kassel.

"It was a complete fiasco," recalls battle veteran George M. Collar.

The Germans, pursuing the main convoy, launched ME-109 Messerschmitt fighter planes—designed to distract American fighters—and slower, more deadly Focke-Wulf 190 storm fighters especially built to pick off bombers.

About 45 miles southeast of Kassel, the 150 German fighters instead came upon the lagging 445th. Within three minutes 25 American bombers were spiraling down in flames. Five more later crashed trying to get home or returned so damaged that they were declared total losses. It was the greatest loss of bombers for any individual group of the 8th Air Force.

During the battle, gunners aboard the bombers and several late-arriving American P-51 fighters managed to down 29 German fighters.

From their B-24, nicknamed "Patches," Newell Brainard and his pilot, Lt. Raphael Carrow, saw the plane in front of them burst into flames. Newell pounded on Carrow's arm—an engine was afire and Germans were bearing down. "Patches" tail assembly had been all but destroyed. A fire spread and the crew was bailing out.

"Brainard was trying to get out, (but) the bomb bay was a roaring inferno," Carrow later wrote a companion. Carrow finally made it to the bomb bay but found only blue sky—the plane had split in two. He had no choice but to leap into the abyss.

Carrow, one of 121 Americans taken as prisoners of war, knew when he bailed out that Newell Brainard was no longer in the plane. But he never learned his copilot's fate. He believed, as did most, that Newell was one of the 118 Americans killed that day as their planes fell in a 20-mile circle around the small town of Bad Hersfeld.

On the ground, a 12-year old boy watched in awe as the explosions formed black clouds in the sky and airmen parachuted to earth. His name was Walter Hassenpflug.

Back in West Palm Beach, Florida, the Brainard family learned that Newell was missing in action.

In November 1944, Kay (who had been secretary to the commander at The Breakers hotel, which had been converted to Ream military hospital) joined the American Red Cross and went to Europe. But there was no further word about her brother.

In September 1945, after he had been missing one year, the army declared Newell Brainard KIA—"killed in action." The family never held a memorial ceremony.

A September 1947 report identifies Newell. He had been buried in March 1946 at the American military cemetery at St. Avold, France, as un-known soldier X-1535. The military used dental records, physical characteristics, and the name "Brainard" found on a wool undershirt on the body to identify him.

It wasn't until April of 1948 that the American military told the family of the identification. They gave no indication that the cause of death was any different from that given earlier—shot down over Germany.

Newell's mother opted to have him remain buried with his comrades.

In later years, Kay became an assistant to actor and part-time Palm Beach resident Douglas Fairbanks, Jr. In the early 1980s, she was a volunteer historian for the 8th Air Force. That led her to Walter Hassenpflug.

The day of the Kassel raid, Hassenpflug and fellow members of the Bad Hersfeld Hitler Youth had scattered into adjoining fields, gathering and burning leaflets and ration cards dropped by the American planes.

Two months later, during an American raid a bomb struck his house, killing his parents.

The drama of the Kassel battle intrigued him in later years, especially when veterans from both sides began visiting the area. He began gathering everything he could about it—interviewing townspeople and contacting veterans' groups and archives from both countries. His efforts intensified in the 1980s with the launching of a project to build a battle memorial.

In April of 1987, Kay Hutchins got a letter from Kassel veteran George Collar, who had seen in a newsletter a note from her asking for details of her brother's death.

Collar attached a copy of the March 1987 letter to him from Walter Hassenpflug in Germany. Kay saw her brother's name.

"It is possible that he landed with his chute near the village of Nentershausen and was one of the five airmen who were shot to death there," Hassenpflug wrote.

"I was horrified," Kay says now. "I owed it to myself to find out."

In March of 1990, Kay was in New York working with Fairbanks. She decided to board a train for the National Archives center near Washington. After spending an entire day in the 8th Air Force files, she was unable to find the report about the Kassel mission. A researcher told her it had been missing since 1970.

As a dejected Kay prepared to leave, the researcher stopped her. He told her that what she really wanted was her brother's burial file. He would find it and send her copies. About a month later, 129 pages arrived.

"Nobody had ever looked past the first page of his file," she says now. "It wasn't until I reached page 80 that the story began to gel."

The September 17, 1947 burial report—the one that identified Newell Brainard as the body that had been discovered in a mass grave—was a poor copy, but one word on it could be clearly read: "Murdered."

For the Germans, nothing inspired more hate, or glee at the opportunity for vengeance, than a loving, downed American airman.

With American GIs fighting Germans far off at the front, it was the U.S. bombers alone who the Germans saw destroying their factories and towns. And it was the airmen alone whom people could punish when they fell from the sky. But the first Germans to encounter Newell Brainard presented only compassion. They found him lying amid his parachute in a field, suffering a head wound, and they took him to a nearby village, where a Red Cross nurse treated him.

In the next town, the German government ran an *ostarbeitslager*—a labor camp where citizens of eastern European countries were forced to mine copper. Its commanders—under orders to pick up any downed American airmen and hold them for military authorities—quickly learned that some had been captured nearby.

"They were supposed to detain them," says Gunter Lemke, Hassenpflug's interpreter and associate on much of the Kassel battle research. "They took it on their own to murder these people."

One pilot was shot in town; the other four, including Newell, were taken to the labor camp. There, the fliers were interrogated and beaten. Finally, they were led outside and shot with pistols. All five were thrown into a single grave in the town cemetery.

Even as the atrocities were taking place, the labor camp's days were numbered. That week the Russians were in the Baltics,

Bulgaria and Yugoslavia; the Allies were marching through the Netherlands. Within months, the war was over, the German Reich destroyed.

Soon after setting up an occupation force, Americans began asking residents about any downed airmen. The townspeople led them to the grave. A February 28, 1945 report on Newell's as-yet-unidentified body said he had been clubbed, then shot. According to reports, the remains had been found in a mattress cover in a box, two bullet holes in his head.

Residents identified suspects. Seven were rounded up; an eighth had committed suicide on the last day of the war.

The Americans set up a war crimes trial that began in June, 1947, in the town of Dachau, site of the infamous concentration camp. The military court ruled that all but one of the seven defendants were eager principals in the beatings or killings and not merely curious bystanders, as each of the accused contended he was.

Three were hanged, one was sentenced to death but had already been hanged for another crime, and the other three were given jail terms.

The camp commanders would have shared all Germans' hatred for airmen, and most were put in such jobs specifically because they were fanatics and were especially cruel, say Hassenpflug and Lemke. But it would be pure speculation to try to place a firm motive on the slayings, the two say.

Kay Hutchins says her brother's murderers were "just mean, I think."

Newell Brainard's mother died in 1957, never knowing how her son really died. There's no way to know after all these years why or how the military never told Brainard's family the circumstances of his death, says Doug Howard, mortuary programs specialist for the U.S. Army. Howard notes that the military did not have the communications setup it does now, but says it would be pure speculation to blame the omission on bureaucracy. There's no evidence that the military had a policy of withholding such details from families, he says.

Kay Hutchins knows her brother's killers paid for their crimes. She also knows that atrocities were committed on both sides: An American soldier admitted to her that he machine-gunned five German prisoners because one called him a swine.

On August 1, 1990, Kay and nearly 80 other Americans traveled to a site deep in the Hesse State Forest in central Germany. On three granite stones, markers detailed the battle of Kassel and listed the 25 German and 118 American airmen who died.

Five hundred Germans joined the Americans for a solemn ceremony. A German Air Force trumpeter played taps. Former enemies shook hands. Prayers were offered.

Kay Hutchins finally met Walter Hassenpflug. Through an interpreter, the two shared the stories of how each had lost loved ones to the war.

The following day, as church bells tolled, Kay Hutchins would see where her brother's plane crashed, where he parachuted down, and the house where a Red Cross nurse had performed an act of mercy later fouled by an act of evil.

But for a moment, there in front of the stark stones, she reached out to touch the brass plate and run her finger over her brother's name.

Author's note: The preceding article, slightly condensed here, originally appeared in The Palm Beach Post on May 31, 1992, written by Post Staff Writer Eliot Kleinberg. George Collar, referred to in the article, was a bombardier on the crew of James Schaen, whose B-24 was also shot down. Collar became a POW, but before he was taken away, Collar was forced to collect all the American dead and wounded in the area. (His story appeared in the Spring 1995 issue of the Journal, page 21).

Of the nine men who were on the crew of Raphael Carrow, five perished either on the plane or upon capture, including the murdered copilot Newell Brainard. Four survived the capture and the war. Since then, all but Carrow have died.

Aside from Newell Brainard, the four additional 445th airmen murdered on that fateful day were John Donahue, of Oliver Elder's crew, and John Cowgill, Hector Scala and James Fields, all of James Baynhams's crew.

Taps—Do You Know
the Whole Story?

Reprinted from The Santa Ana Cadet, Costa Mesa Historical Society

It all began in 1862 during the Civil War, when Union Army Captain Robert Ellicombe was with his men near Harrison's Landing in Virginia. The Confederate Army was on the other side of the narrow strip of land. During the night, Captain Ellicombe heard the moans of a soldier who lay mortally wounded on the field. Not knowing if it was a Union or Confederate soldier, the Captain decided to risk his life and bring the stricken man back for medical attention.

Crawling on his stomach through the gunfire, the Captain reached the stricken soldier and began pulling him toward his encampment. When the Captain finally reached his own lines, he discovered it was actually a Confederate soldier but the soldier was dead.

The Captain lit a lantern and suddenly caught his breath and went numb with shock. In the dim light, he saw the face of the soldier. It was his own son. The boy had been studying music in the South when the war broke out. Without telling his father, he enlisted in the Confederate Army.

The following morning, heartbroken, the father asked permission of his superiors to give his son a full military burial despite his enemy status. His request was only partially granted. The Captain had asked if he could have a group of Army band members play a funeral dirge for his son at the funeral. The request was turned down since the soldier was a Confederate but out of respect for the father, they did say they could give him one musician.

The Captain chose a bugler. He asked the bugler to play a series of musical notes he had found on a piece of paper in the pocket of the dead youth's uniform. This wish was granted. The haunting melody we now know as "Taps" used at military funerals was born.

Author's note: fact or fiction? Either way it's a heck of a story.

SNAFU – B-17 Style

Reprinted from Yankee Wings.

"Snafu" –a word which originated during World War II—is defined as "confusion" or "muddle." It evolved from the acronym, Situation Normal, All Fouled Up.

It was another mission that began on a dark morning for the 390th Bombardment Group, 8th Air Force at Framlingham. Colonel Wittan, the Group Operations Officer, and L. Col. Tom Jeffrey, the Air Executive, stood on the control tower awaiting the signal to start the mission. When the green flare fired, B-17s would begin taxiing from their hardstands toward the runway. They would proceed in order of takeoff to end where the first six aircraft would take staggered positions on the runway, with the rest strung out on the perimeter road to facilitate a 30-second takeoff spacing.

At this moment, the engineering officer reported that the lead ship was still at its hardstand with a flat tailwheel tire. Col. Wittan immediately ordered that the No. 2 aircraft lead the takeoff and climb out to the assembly point at 18,000 feet; however, with radio silence in force, he turned to Lt. Col. Jeffrey:

"Take my staff car . . . to the end of the runway and tell the pilot of No. 2 to lead the group up to assembly altitude."

Jeffrey sped away and pulled the car off the runway to the right rear of the aircraft so he could enter it through the rear door without crossing in front of the propellers (Ed. Note: B-24s did not have a rear door). Leaving the car's engine running and lights on, he bolted for the bomber, opened the door and jumped in. Just as he scrambled on board, the pilot gunned the engines and released the brakes. Jeffrey yelled, but nobody heard him over the roar of the engines. Wearing his summer flight suit, he moved easily through the confines of the bomber; however, by the time he reached the cockpit it was too late to abort the takeoff. When the landing gear was up and the aircraft was under control, he reached over and tapped the pilot's shoulder.

"What the hell are you doing here?" the surprised pilot asked.

"It's a long story," Jeffrey replied, "but let's keep going until we're organized."

As they climbed and circled, getting the formation pulled together, Jeffrey started to get cold in his summer flying suit. He had no jacket, parachute, or oxygen mask either, and the aircraft was scheduled to fly to Germany. Short of completing the round trip, there were only two ways to get him back on the ground—the aircraft could abort, or he could bail out. As the Fortress continued to circle around the assembly point at 18,000 feet, a shivering Lt. Col. Jeffrey gulped oxygen from a walk-around bottle. Soon the group lead arrived, and the No. 2 assumed station on his wing.

Now what? Would Jeffrey go to Germany and Freeze half to death en route? What if they were hit? How would he get out? Should he order the pilot to abort?

Fortunately, fate intervened. Radio silence was broken by a recall order—stormy weather over the target would interfere with accurate bombing. The 390th airmen gave silent cheers, but none more fervently than Jeffrey. Still, they carried a full load of fuel and bombs, so they had to circle for four hours before enough fuel had burned off to enable the aircraft to land safely with the bombs on board.

When the aircraft reached its hardstand, a chastened Lt. Col. Jeffrey returned to the quarters that he shared with Colonel Wittan. Having awakened at 2 a.m. to plan the briefing, the colonel was just waking up from a nap when his air exec entered.

"Jeff, will you please tell me where the hell you've been? And why did you leave my car at the end of the runway with the engine running and the lights on?"

Looking at the colonel, Jeffrey replied, "Well, Colonel, I'll tell you, it was like this..."

Auf Wiedersehen

Ken "Deacon" Jones (389th)

Letter orders of the 389th Bombardment Group (H) set up the first Trolley Mission the group flew on 3 May 1945.

These tours were a belated recognition of the vital and invaluable services provided by ground support personnel in bringing the war to a successful conclusion.

The pre-dawn briefing held that morning revealed this first aerial tour of war-torn Germany would get to land on the German border at Y-55, an advance base at Venlo, Holland. Army trucks would transport visitors to the heavily bombed cities of Cologne and Dusseldorf for walking tours.

The sightseeing bombers would fly individually. We were one minimum flight crew of four, with 16 ground support people as passengers. Nazi fanatics were still active. We were issued helmets, firearms, K-rations, canteens and two blankets. The .45 cal. pistol in a shoulder holster was the deodorant prescribed by the Army Air Force for some of us and others had carbines.

The weather set the overall mood for this special flight—cold, dreary, and bleak.

I noted that although the war was not officially over, the 8th A.F. ran out of targets in April. The Allied ground forces were busy rounding up the last remnants of the Wehrmacht armies in now mostly occupied Germany.

No one could have adequately prepared us for the big picture we were going to see—the massive destruction of aerial bombing and hundreds of thousands of German prisoners behind barbed wire fences without shelter of any kind.

The sameness of the scenery of sunken barges, collapsed bridges, including the Ludendorff Bridge at Remagen, the shredded devastation of a torn landscape littered with burned-out military vehicles and the shocking view of leveled cities became monotonous as we became immune to the savagery of war. You knew what the next town would look like before you came to it.

Going south, we passed over Duren, Germany on the way out. Another pulverized town. No roofs or ceilings intact; only jagged walls. We left behind the ruin that was Germany and turned west to Liege, Belgium and the coast. A silence came over the occupants of a front line military bomber called "The Liberator."

The feeling of a door closing behind you came as the city of Ostende went astern for the last time. We pointed the nose across the Channel for England, flying smoothly under a low ceiling and leaden skies, into dim light and home. We landed at Hethel, in the quiet of the evening, at 18:00 hours.

Epilogue

When I first thought about an epilogue, I wondered what it should contain. I have a multitude of curiosities, and the principal one is people. No two the same, all have something interesting to tell.

What made my life pleasant and happy: wonderful parents and sisters; growing up on the prairie; serving my country in time of need; college; falling in love with Ann; having four rewarding children; the challenge and success in finder/intermediary activity; starting and managing a family business and growing it to a sizable, profitable, fun enterprise; traveling extensively, U.S. and abroad; and retirement at age 87 and the time to formulate this effort.

Have I made the world a better place? It's not worse because of me. I recognize that's not enough.

I've discovered that the writings are never finished. You think of passages to improve, and delete others that don't sound as good as when written. But—at some point it must go to the printer, short of what you consider your best effort.

Even with a few aches, pains, and maladies, living is a gift. BE POSITIVE AND ENJOY IT!

From a song:

Adieu, adieu kind friends,
adieu,
I can no longer stay with you...

Photos and Maps
From the Author's
Collection

This is my favorite airplane to fly. AT-6. The Texan. 650 h.p. Maneuverable Retractable Gear. Trainer for Air Force and Navy. 2 Capacity. Navy's designation (?).

*My WWII buddy, Joe Shogan, first pilot 8th Air Force
from near Donara, Pennsylviania.*

Escaped with a bit of trouble in the #2 engine.

Brunswick.

The author and a friend.

Crashed in desert. Damaged or out of gas.

Far Left (back row) Author. Far Right (back row) Isidore Buechner (from "Issy was a Hero").